s

Breathtaking

Rainbows

Harro Hieronimus

We would like to thank the following specialists, companies, breeders and hobbyists for their advice and kindly letting us use their slides. We also thank all those we might have forgotten.

G. R. Allen, N. Armstrong, D. Bork, H.-G. Evers, N. Grunwald, R. Kuiter, G. W. Lange, G. Maebe, W. Maleck, M. & C. Piednoir, G. Schmida, E. Schraml, G. Stables, F. Teigler, W. A. Tomey, U. Werner

Aquarium Glaser GmbH,
for providing beautiful fish for our photographers from their weekly imports.

amtra - **Aquaristik GmbH,**
for providing furnished aquaria and equipment for testing.

Veterinary consultant:
Dr. med. vet. Markus Biffar,
veterinarian, fish specialist

Further useful tips about care and maintenance can be found every six weeks in **AQUALOG*news***, the unique newspaper for all friends of the hobby.

Read, for example, the latest breeding reports in the *news*. It is available in German or English and can be obtained at your local pet shop or subscribed to at the publisher.

Order your free specimen copy!

Die Deutsche Bibliothek - CIP-Einheitsaufnahme
AQUALOG: *Special* - **Serie Ratgeber**
Mörfelden-Walldorf: A.C.S.
Breathtaking Rainbows – 1999

Breathtaking Rainbows
Harro Hieronimus

ISBN 3-931702-51-0
NE: Hieronimus, Harro

© **Copyright by:**   **AQUALOG** Verlag GmbH
Rothwiesenring 5
D-64546 Mörfelden-Walldorf
Germany

Author: Harro Hieronimus

Editor:
Dipl. Biol. Frank Schäfer

Cover Layout:
Gabriele Geiß, Büro für Grafik, Frankfurt a.M.

Pront typesetting, processing:
Lithographics: Frank Teigler/AQUALOG Verlag GmbH
Layout: Bettina Kirsch/AQUALOG Verlag GmbH
          and Harro Hieronimus
Print: Giese-Druck, Offenbach
Printed on EURO ART
100% chlorine free paper

Editors address:
AQUALOG Verlag GmbH
Liebigstraße 1
D-63110 Rodgau
Telephone: +49 (0) 6106 – 64 46 91
Fax: +49 (0) 6106 – 64 46 92

e-mail: acs@aqualog.de
http://www.aqualog.de

PRINTED IN GERMANY

Cover Photos:
upper left: Melanotaenia trifasciata, Goyder River
(Photo: Richter/Archiv A.C.S.)
upper right: Pseudomugil connieae (Photo: Richter/Archiv A.C.S.)
below: Melanotaenia boesemani (Photo: Migge/Archiv A.C.S.)
page 2/3: Melanotaenia trifasciata, Goyder River
(Photo: G. Schmida)

Acknowledgements

This book could not have been written without the participation and help of several aquarists and scientists. I am especially indebted to Dr. Gerald R. Allen who generously shared his knowledge with me and answered several questions. Gilbert Maebe and Norbert Grunwald are only two of the breeders – representative for many members of the International Rainbowfish Association IRG – who let me participate in their rich experience and who enriched my knowledge also by critical reviews and comments. I cannot mention all the others at this place but the ones will know that it's them I think of here. I also have to mention the members of the Rainbowfish Mailing List in the internet, where I also received several useful informations and contacts. For the help with the translation of the text I thank Dr. Bruce Hansen, Dean Scott, Michael Eckardt and Tsuh Yang Chen.

Numerous photographs have contributed to the success of this book project. I just want to name – in alphabetical order – Dr. Gerald R. Allen, Neil Armstrong, Dieter Bork, Norbert Grunwald, Rudie H. Kuiter, Gary W. Lange, Gilbert Maebe, M. & C. Piednoir, Gunther Schmida, and W. A. Tomey. My special thanks to them.

I don't want to pass the chance to thank Mr. Ulrich Glaser sen. for the possibility of the realisation of this project and Frank Schäfer for his generous help.

Last but not least I have to thank Gisela, my wife, who supported me by relieve me of several of my normal duties and thus made it possible to write this book.

Content

	page
Presentation of the author	6
Preface	7

History and geography:

The discovery of the rainbowfish and the blue-eyes	8
The systematic position of the rainbowfish	9
The aquaristic history of the rainbowfish	10
Evolution of rainbowfish and atherinid fish	12

Biotopes:

The home of the rainbowfish	13
The home of blue-eyes and atherinid fish	14

General maintenance:

Aquarium and decoration	15
The proper water	17
The proper diet	18

Reproduction:

Breeding preparations	20
The breeding	22
Raising the fry	25
Special breeding features	26

	page

Diseases:

The quarantine-aquarium	27
Diagnosis and treatment	28
Bacterial infections	29
Intestinal diseases and poisoning	30

The fishes:

Rainbowfishes	31
Other atheriniform fishes	35
Local varieties	38
Breeding forms and threatened species	39
Local varieties and Breeding Forms	40
Threatened species	41

The AQUALOG system:

Information and description	42

The fishes:

New species	44

Further informations:

Literature	46
Glossary	46
Index	47
Symbols	48

Presentation of the Author

Harro Hieronimus

It must have been in 1983 when he saw the first specimens of *Melanotaenia boesemani* in a local petshop. It must have been the offspring of the specimens imported in 1982 for the first time. Wonderful fishes, but far too expensive for him as he still was a student at that time. Thus he saw them in the dealer's tank but didn't have any rainbowfish yet.

Accordingly other fish played the main role in his aquaria at that time. Motive for his further occupation with rainbowfish actually was an annoyance. In 1985 he became interested in one of the smaller representatives of these pretty fishes. However, although seaking intensively he did not succeed in finding more than males of the wonderful Threadfin Rainbowfish *Iriatherina werneri*. There seemed to practically not exist any females. Then he tried to read everything which had been published in German aquarium magazines about rainbowfish up to then and found that it wasn't much yet. Several articles of Dr. Juergen CLASEN were surely worth reading and informative, but that's were he ended up with. However, it seemed to be a very interesting group of fish. But he still hadn't found the sought after female *I. werneri* although he meanwhile had found some other rainbowfish enthusiasts. It should take some more time until he finally had his female Threadfin Rainbowfish.

It must have been about the same time when *Melanotaenia herbertaxelrodi* was imported. Some time this fish was available in the better assorted petshops but then vanished within short time. Harro Hieronimus now purchased the book of ALLEN & CROSS (see literature) and learned that the rainbowfish were a larger group of fish with partially unbelievable colourful species. But unfortunately it was nearly impossible to obtain the different species. Additionally no rainbowfish club existed in Europe. Thus he initiated the foundation of the International Rainbowfish Association e. V. (IRG) in 1986 in Duesseldorf/ Germany. Since that time he also is in chair of the IRG. Soon members of the IRG imported numerous species of rainbowfish. Two members have to be mentioned in the first row: Heiko BLEHER and Gilbert MAEBE, who imported most species of rainbowfish and blue-eyes to Europe for the first time. It was the duty of the other members of the IRG to preserve these species for our aquaria by breeding them. With the "Rainbowfish" the most important European magazine on this matter was founded. It is published since 1986, meanwhile with four annual issues in three different languages, German, English and Dutch. Additionally there are good contacts with the rainbowfish clubs in Australia and the U.S.

While his scientific works concentrates on some other groups of fish – which may be the description of new species or behavioural studies – the rainbowfish take his fascination by their bright colours and their vivid behaviour.

In his numerous aquaria he keeps different species of rainbowfish, blue-eyes and atherinid fish. By his lectures he tries to propagate this part of his hobby not only in Germany but throughout nearly the whole of Europe. You may also contact him and learn more about IRG:

H. Hieronimus
Postfach 170209
D-42624 Solingen
eMail: irg@hieronimus.de

Wolfgang Glaser

Boeseman's Rainbow-fish, Melanotaenia boesemani, male in normal colouration. (Photo: G. Schmida)

Preface

Australia and especially New Guinea form not only the continent which has been discovered as last one. Also science started relatively late exploring the animals, and even today nearly every year new species are discovered, not only on New Guinea as the difficult to survey second largest island of the world.

Since more than ten years rainbowfish are an important part of aquarism. Not just our knowledge about these fish has greatly enlarged during this time, also the number of species – as well of species which have been newly discovered or rediscovered in nature but also of imported and thus available aquarium fish – has strongly increased. With several species belonging to the standard assortment of pet-shops also the number of keepers grew strongly. Meanwhile rainbowfish belong to the most popular aquarium fishes.

In this connection it is very important that many of the species are not only easy to keep but also easy to breed. Beside their striking colouration it are peaceful fishes, thus nearly ideal aquarium fishes, and many of them also apologize the typical mistakes beginners make. Additionally their nutrition – with some exceptions – is very easy. So you may find species for beginners, and also ones for experienced aquarists, e.g. those who need a special diet.

This book has been written chiefly for aquarists which haven't had contact with rainbowfish very intensively. On the one hand it shall offer all basic information which is necessary for the successful maintenance and breeding of rainbowfishes. On the other hand, however, it shall also encourage the interested aquarist to let the fishes have a suitable and species specific care to preserve the species in our aquaria. Unfortunately today even the most remote parts of the world are not safe against the devastation of the environment and wasteful exploitation, more and more fishes are already today solely existing in our aquaria, among them also some rainbowfish. With the conservation of a small part of nature in our homes aquarists took over an important duty.

For a long time the blue-eyes belonged to the rainbowfish. Although this book also deals with these fish, every time I write rainbowfishes the real rainbowfishes are meant with the blue-eyes not belonging to them. There are too many differences in keeping and breeding the members of these two families also if they co-exist in several habitats. Also the atherinid fishes are closely related to the rainbowfish and blue-eyes. But, as only some of them occur in fresh water and only few of them have ever been kept in aquaria, this book deals with them only in part. The cultivation of the more wellknown species, however, is rather similar to that of the rainbow-fish, so all aquarists interested in these fish may have an orientation in the advice for keeping and breeding these fish. Nevertheless all of the related families are presented in the AQUALOG-Lexicon "all atherinids" where you also can find nearly all of the rainbowfishes and blue-eyes known until today as well as many atheriniform fishes together with details on their systematics.

By the way, there is no aquarium for which you can't find suitable rainbowfish or blue-eyes. If you have a small or a very large aquarium, you can always find a species which perfectly fits, the scale reaches between 3 cm and 20 cm fish length. While the small species are better kept in an aquarium on their own, the larger species make ideal fishes for the community aquarium, suitable to be kept with other fishes, which only have to be as peaceful as the rainbowfish are.

One of the most important characteristics an aquarist should have who wants to engage in the rainbowfish hobby is patience. You need it for two reasons. First of all, to get the required fish as only few species are offered, but second to see them grow to adultness. Unfortunately most of the rainbowfish grow very slowly and, un-fortunately, do not show their brightest colours before they are nearly adult. The latter point is the main reason for the fact that only few species are offered in the commercial trade as fishes, which have to be fed a whole year before you can sell them are of course not really a bargain, and the younger, "grey" specimens are hard to sell.

However, whoever invests this patience will be rewarded with some of the most colourful and outstanding aquarium fishes I know.

Harro Hieronimus

History and Geography
The Discovery of the Rainbowfish and the Blue-Eyes

The scientific discovery of the rainbowfishes

The first Australian settlers had other problems than to worry about the fish world. During colonization the places which could be reached by ship played a very prominent role, as because of the great desert in the central parts and the desert in the southwest many areas couldn't be reached in any other way.

Thus it is not astonishing that the first scientifically described rainbowfish was caught in Port Essington in the Northern Territory – by the way by angling. This fish was described in 1843 by RICHARDSON as *Atherina nigrans*. Already in 1862 the American ichthyologist GILL realized the independent role of this fish group, erected the subfamily Melanotaeniinae and placed *Melanotaenia nigrans* as the first species into it. The generic name means black lined and is related to the prominent dark lateral body stripe many rainbowfishes show.

However, thereafter it took more than 100 years before the Australian scientist Ian S. R. MUNRO erected the family Melanotaeniidae for these fish and 25 years more before the Pseudomugilidae were placed in a family of its own. The present status is controversial. However, in this book I will follow the opinion chiefly expressed by IVANTSOFF and co-authors.

The first blue-eyes

It was left to the Austrians to describe the first blue-eye scientifically. The Austrian frigate "Novara" in the early years of last century's 60s had the duty to sail around the world and, amongst others, collect fishes. The Austrian ichthyologist Rudolf KNER described the newly found species in 1865 as *Pseudomugil signifer*, the generic name meaning "false mugilid" and thus pointing towards the close relationship to the Mugilidae.

The phases of discovery in rainbowfishes and blue-eyes

In the discovery history of rainbowfishes and blue-eyes there are a few phases where many species were discovered and named. The first of these phases occurred in the western part of New Guinea, which was Dutch until the middle of the 1950s and now belongs to Indonesia (Irian Jaya). In the beginning of this century two Dutch scientists, Max WEBER and Lieven F. DE BEAUFORT, explored today's Indonesia. Principally WEBER discovered, described and named several rainbowfishes and blue-eyes. If you remember that even today it is said that in the most remote areas of Irian Jaya cannibals still occur, this must have been a dangerous and difficult job.

Since the middle of the 50s to the end of the 60s MUNRO engaged himself in detail with the Australian and later with the New Guinean fish fauna. We have to thank him for, among others, the description of the Lake Kutubu or Blue Rainbowfish, *Melanotaenia lacustris*.

Since 1974 Gerald R. ALLEN, who until recently was the curator of fishes at the Western Australian Museum in Perth, has been involved with these fishes. He has succeeded in more than doubling the number of known rainbowfishes by the description of new species. Since 1998 he is more often working in Irian Jaya and is still finding new species. With the description of new blue-eyes and in work and descriptions on the Australian hardyheads (atherinid fishes of the genus *Craterocephalus*), he often co-operated with Walter IVANTSOFF from Macquarie University, Sydney, Australia.

More aquaristically relevant aquarium fishes

Only a few fishes of the order of atheriniform fishes (Atheriniformes) to which the rainbowfishes belong are amongst the species kept in aquaria at least from time to time. Beside the hardyheads we have to mention the popular Celebes Rainbowfish, *Marosatherina ladigesi* (formerly *Telmatherina*), described in 1936 by the Berlin ichthyologist Ernst AHL.

On Madagascar we find some atheriniform fishes of the family Bedotiidae. Most of them were described by the French ichthyologist Jacques PELLEGRIN. In recent times Melanie J. STIASSNY and Paul V. LOISELLE have been working with these fish. One of these species is rather well known under the name *Bedotia geayi*, Madagascar Rainbow. However, it seems to be another species. More on that matter in the AQUALOG-Lexicon "all atherinid fishes".

As opposed to their common names in Germany, *Marosatherina ladigesi* and *Bedotia geayi* are called "rainbowfishes". Although closely related, they clearly show systematic differences. Therefore you shouldn't mix them with the real rainbowfishes, the Melanotaeniidae.

The rainbowfishes in the system of fishes

As well as the rainbowfishes, the blue-eyes belong to the order Atheriniformes, the

The Systematic Position of the Rainbowfish

atheriniform fishes. All aquaristically well known fishes belong to the superfamily Atherinoidea. Because of some systematic characteristics the Bedotiidae and Melanotaeniidae are recognized as closely related. A close, but not as close relationship exists between the Pseudomugilidae and the Telmatherinidae – not astonishing if you remember that one representative of the Telmatherinidae has originally been described as a *Pseudomugil* species and until today is known as the only New Guinean representative of the family Telmatherinidae. Apart from that, this family is only known from the island of Celebes (Sulawesi). The other atherinid fishes of the family Atherinidae are positioned between the rainbowfishes and blue-eyes.

Example:
The classification of *Melanotaenia boesemani* in the system of species

Class	Osteichthyes Bonyfishes
Superorder	Teleostei Real Bonyfishes
Series	Atherinomorpha Atheriniform related fishes
Order	Atheriniformes Atheriniform fishes
Superfamily	Atherinoidea Real atheriniform fishes
Family	Melanotaeniidae Real rainbowfishes
Genus	Melanotaenia
Species	Melanotaenia boesemani

In the blue-eyes – Pseudomugilidae – additionally three subfamilies are described, Kiunginae, Pseudomugilinae and Scaturiginichthyinae.
Behind the specific name you often (e. g. in the AQUALOG-Lexicon) find the name of the original first describers. If these names are listed in brackets, the fish have originally been described under another generic name, like in *Melanotaenia nigrans* (RICHARDSON, 1843).
In total seven families with 56 genera and some 300 species belong to the order Atheriniformes. Among these 10 genera and some 80 species belong to the rainbowfishes and blue-eyes.

Rainbowfishes:	
Cairnsichthys:	1 species
Chilatherina:	10 species
Glossolepis:	7 species
Iriatherina:	1 species
Melanotaenia:	44 species
Pelangia:	1 species
Rhadinocentrus:	1 species
Blue-eyes:	
Kiunga:	1 species
Pseudomugil:	14 species
Scaturiginichthys:	1 species

In summary there are 81 species. However, you have to add many more distinguishable varieties and some still undescribed species. Still today, most of all in the difficult to reach remote parts of New Guinea, new species are awaiting discovery based on present experience. Even in Australia there are species which have been known for years, but which don't exactly fit in with the known species and which may accordingly represent new species in some future revision.

Characteristics of the rainbowfishes

Typical characteristics of the rainbowfishes as well as their closer relatives are the large eye, the deeply forked mouth, the two dorsal fins, the first having less rays but sometimes having longer fin rays, and the rather long anal fin. A more or less prominent black band (which may be silvery in some of the related species) runs through the middle two scale rows, from the gill cover or even from the snout down to the tail.
Many more rainbowfish characteristics may only be seen in a detailed examination and shall only be mentioned in the following as examples. Several of these characteristics deal with the shape and the dentition of the jaws, the arrangement of the vertebrae as well as the bones of the body and the skull. They are of less use for the determination of the species as they differ not very much among these but can be used to determine the relations between the different genera and families. The species themselves may be distinguished and characterized by bodyshape and scale and fin ray counts. In contrast to these the colour (for the normal aquarist a very important distinguishing criterion), is less important for the scientific determination of the species which is in large part due to the fact that most of the rainbowfish are dead when examined scientifically.

History and Geography
The Aquaristic History of the Rainbowfish

The rainbowfish imported to Germany and maybe Europe as first of his family may have been Melanotaenia duboulayi. The photo shows two males from Kangaroo Creek near Tin Can Bay, Queensland. (Photo: G. Schmida)

The aquaristic history of the rainbowfishes, outside Australia, started in the year 1927 when a German aquarist named Amandus RUDEL emigrated to Australia, settled near Brisbane and joined an aquarium club. In Germany he had been used to the tropical imported fishes, most coming from South America, thus he wanted to have them also in Australia. To find a way to get some he contacted the editor-in-chief of the German aquarist magazine "Wochenschrift für Aquarien- und Terrarienkunde" and soon a first exchange of Australian for South American fishes took place. Only one pair survived the very long transport to Germany, but were easily bred in large numbers. The fish had been identified as *Melanotaenia nigrans,* a mistake which remained in the aquarium literature until the middle of the 70s when the real *M. nigrans* where imported first to Germany. Probably these first fishes were *M. duboulayi* as far as can be determined today.

The Dwarf Rainbowfish, Melanotaenia maccullochi. That should have been the look of the fishes imported first. (Photo: H. Hieronimus)

Astonishingly enough their impact was relatively small. The German aquarists took notice of the newly imported fishes but they seemed to be too poorly coloured for them (surely it was a less colourful variety than the photo above) and somewhat too robust. Also the fact that they were easy to breed was surely no challenge. However, this changed in 1934 when the second species, *Melanotaenia maccullochi,* was imported. This rainbowfish was named the Dwarf Rainbowfish – in contrast *M. duboulayi* was named Great Rainbowfish – and soon was widely distributed. Even during World War II and the difficult time after the war in Germany some of the stocks were persistently kept. Since its first introduction it belonged to the occasionally offered species list of the pet trade, not only in Germany.

1936 saw *Pseudomugil signifer* as the first blue-eye imported to Germany. However, it appeared that it was much more difficult to keep and breed than the rainbowfishes and thus did not have a long career at that time. Additionally, it was the short-finned variety (see page 11 bottom), the large-fin variety had not been imported until a few years ago and surely would have attracted greater attention even in former times.

In 1973 and 1974 *Iriatherina werneri* and *Glossolepis incisus,* two more rainbowfishes, found their way into our aquaria. It was the private inititiative of J. CLASEN, Siegburg, that brought some more Australian species to Germany in 1976. But also in other countries the rainbowfishes lived in the shadow, even in Australia they hadn't found more than a handful of friends at that time.

History and Geography
The Aquaristic History of the Rainbowfish

The Pacific Blue-eye, under which name *Pseudomugil signifer* is also kept, has a very large distribution. In some parts of the spread there are populations with strongly extended fins, e.g. in Harvey Creek. (Photo: G. Schmida)

This changed in the beginning of the 80s. ALLEN & CROSS published a book on the rainbowfishes of Australia and Papua New Guinea which for the first time showed the variety of species and their bright colours. On the other hand it was at that time when Heiko BLEHER imported *Melanotaenia boesemani* – accompanied by suitable advertising –, one of the most popular rainbowfishes of New Guinea even today. Within short intervals new species were continually added to the list, with examples like *M. lacustris* and *M. praecox* making their way in the pet shop trade. *M. praecox*, the Neon Rainbowfish, which already had been described in 1910 but had not been rediscovered by ALLEN until 1991.

By the initiative of several members of the IRG and also the other societies where rainbow-fishfriends have gathered, several more species were introduced into Europe and the USA. As Australia in the early 80's enacted an import prohibition on species from New Guinea, today we have the paradoxical situation that in Europe and the States more rainbowfish species are kept than in Australia. So meanwhile more than 100 different species and colour varieties are kept in Europe alone. However, even the Australians still find new varieties and even new species in their country.

left: Harvey Creek in Queensland. (Photo: G. Stables)

below: The fish imported in 1936 may have looked like this blue-eye from Brisbane River, Queensland. (Photo: G. Schmida)

Evolution of of Rainbowfish and Atherinid Fish

Melanotaeniidae

The Australian continent was separated from the original continent Gondwanaland millions of years ago. At that time the development of the modern freshwater fishes hadn't yet begun. Therefore there are only very few fishes in Australia whose ancestors already at that time lived in freshwater. Accordingly most of the recent Australian fishes originate from species which emigrated from the sea, they are termed secondary freshwater fishes.

Unfortunately the history of the rainbowfishes can not (yet) be demonstrated by fossils. So it is speculated that the ancestors of today's rainbowfishes emigrated into the freshwater about 200,000 years ago. About that time there was a larger glacial period, with the result that the sea level was about 200 m lower than it is today. As a result the Arafura Sea between Australia and New Guinea was dry land at that time. On maps of the sea bottom which also show the so-called continental shelf area you can still recognize the old river beds.

When the glacial period ended the freshwater fish populations on New Guinea, the islands on the shelf area and those in Australia were gradually separated from each other by the rising sea levels. The last ice-age ended about 10,000 years ago, since that period the populations on Australia and the islands are separated finally.

Thus the rainbowfishes seem to be a rather young family whose species evolution is not yet finished. Overall it shows a considerable genetic plasticity with the result that in the relatively short period of just 10,000 years several varieties have developed and maybe even new species. This process seems not to be finished even today, and what is accepted by today's scientists just as a colour variety may be described by later generations as separate species. Today, for example we know about 40 different varieties of *Melanotaenia trifasciata* from the different rivers and creeks of northern Australia which can be distinguished by colour and shape. In *Melanotaenia splendida* not less than five subspecies have been described up to the present time.

However, we additionally know a lot more colour varieties of which many are shown in the AQUALOG-Lexicon.

Pseudomugilidae

In contrast to the real rainbowfishes it is not yet clear when the blue-eyes have developed. On the one hand the family contains species which still today at least partially live in sea water. This enhances the species to exchange genes by passing the seawater barrier. On the other hand several of the characters seem to be younger. That might be a hint for the conclusion that blue-eyes have a somewhat shorter evolutionary history than rainbowfishes have.

Atherinidae

Several atherinid fishes of the family Atherinidae live in freshwater, and even some of the typical seawater species form freshwater populations or migrate at least occasionally into the freshwater from the estuaries. So the representatives of the Australian/Oceanic genus *Craterocephalus* are pure freshwater fishes. It is thought that this genus has a similar age like the Melanotaeniidae. However, the other atherinid fishes are surely older, speaking in evolutionary terms.

Bedotiidae

Although the members of this family are only found on an island – Madagascar – very far away from Australia, where they are endemic (i. e. occuring only there), the Bedotiidae show several similarities to the rainbowfishes and seem to be closely related.

However, you can only suppose that they developed in a similar period. More recent scientific results seem to show that also the bedotiid fishes are very variable. For more details see the AQUALOG-Lexicon.

Telmatherinidae

This family is endemic to Sulawesi (Celebes) (with one exception, see above). There are no hints about the time the family developed.

Phallostethidae

The aquaristically unknown phallostethid fishes seem to be younger species.

Dentatherinidae

As known from fossils aged about 50 million years this seem to be the oldest representative within the rainbowfish relationship.

Rainbowfishes of Australia

Rainbowfishes inhabit nearly all suitable Australian habitats and often are the fishes which occur in the largest numbers in comparism to other species. In the south the distribution in the Murray/Darling system reaches past the Sydney vicinity into Victoria and even into South

Biotopes
The Home of the Rainbowfish

Australia. Queensland in the north-eastern part of Australia is an area with a high diversity of species, similarly across the north. In the north-western parts of Australia you can only find a few species. Part of the distribution of *Melanotaenia splendida australis* may also be found isolated by deserts in the south-western part of Australia.

Although many (mostly the older and not very detailed) books spread the information that rainbowfishes are typical hardwater fishes, in Australia we normally find just the opposite. Factually most of the habitats indeed have soft and slightly acidic water, and a pH value of more than 7 is an exception. Only a few species really come from harder water with a pH value distinctly over 7. The very popular *Melanotaenia trifasciata* variety from Goyder River is said to belong to those species, as well as the *M. maccullochi* introduced first to Germany. Why you should keep rainbowfishes better in hard water is explained in more details in the chapter "Maintainence".

The temperature requirement varies strongly with the origin. In the southernmost part of the distribution area temperatures down to 10°C (50°F) may be reached in the Australian winter, while in the tropical north temperatures between 22°C (72°F) and sometimes more than 30°C (86°F) are typical, also varying with the season.

In many parts of their naturally inhabited waters, few real waterplants occur. Thus often for spawning purposes rainbowfishes and blue-eyes use grass hanging into the water and algae as well as fine tree roots.

Most of all in the eastern parts of Australia heavy seasonal rainfalls occur. The changes of the water values in the course of this additional and sudden water supply are not well documented, but you can suppose that the low pH value will rise slightly, while the hardness will drop down a little.

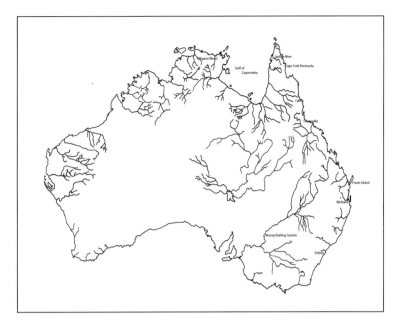

Map of Australia with the most important rivers. Not all of the inland rivers are permanent waters.

Rainbowfishes of New Guinea

New Guinea is amongst the regions of the earth with the most rainfall. Accordingly many of the waters – most of all the smaller ones – undergo strong oscillations in the water levels. In the central mountains area the rivers have a strong current, while in the lowland plains the rivers are broad and slowly running. The special geomorphological surface of New Guinea with its strongly serrated

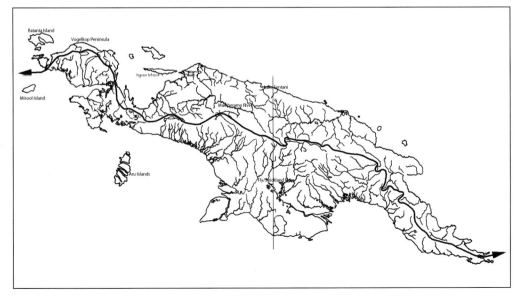

Map of New Guinea. The vertical line shows the political border between Irian Jaya (in the west) and Papua New Guinea. The other line shows the central watershed. (from Allen & Cross, changed)

Biotopes
The Home of Blue-Eyes and Atherinid Fish

above: Male Melanotaenia nigrans, Scotts Creek. (Photo: N. Armstrong) middle: Male Salmonred Rainbowfish, Glossolepis incisus. (Photo: N. Armstrong) below: Male of the hardyhead Craterocephalus stramineus. (Photo: G. Schmida) right: Marosatherina ladigesi, the Celebes Rainbowfish. (Photo: U. Werner)

seasonal changes. Remember the equator crosses this island. But nevertheless not all waters have the same temperature as might be expected, as the differences are caused by the height. As rainbowfishes occur in waters up to 1,600 m elevation, the temperature scale varies from 18°C (64°F) to nearly 30°C (86°F).

Blue-eyes
With one exception – *Scaturiginichthys vermeilipinnis* –blue-eyes occur in the areas close to the coast. Some of them live partially, others nearly constantly in brackish or even seawater. The pH value of these waters may be very different, according to the salt content, and may reach from the slightly acidic waters of the pure freshwater up to more than 8 in waters with a high salt content or pure seawater. In many areas the salt content differs with the tides or also after heavy rainfalls, with the result that these fish easily adapt to various strongly changing water conditions. More on this under "Maintainence" and "Breeding"

Atherinidae
Because of the large distribution of the family only a few species from Australia and New Guinea shall be mentioned. As they often occur together with rainbowfishes, these conditions are also applicable for the hardyheads, *Craterocephalus*. However, there is one exception. As far as we know today, *Craterocephalus stramineus* generally originates from harder waters.

Bedotiidae
Only little is known about the natural waters on Madagascar. These fish are inhabitants of harder waters. The temperatures change only little seasonally, but the members of the genus *Bedotia* are chiefly found in the lowlands (22–28°C, 72–82°F), while *Rheocles* seems to prefer the rivers or lakes which are close to the mountains (18–22°C, 64–72°F).

mountainous areas has led to the formation of several natural lakes which often exhibit endemic rainbowfish and other fish species.

Nearly all of the waters have a pH between 7 and 8, mostly between 7. 2 and 7. 5. Although there are no further waterchemical examinations one can suppose that the water must be somewhat harder than in Australia. However, exceptions are the lakes and rivers of the Vogelkop Peninsula, which are soft and slightly acidic. Also in New Guinea the water conditions change seasonally. One species – *Glossolepis mulitsquamatus* – is known to spawn deliberately in the flooded plains of the rivers on grass leaves.

In contrast to Australia the water temperatures of the New Guinean waters don't show noticable

View into an attractively decorated community aquarium with Melanotaenia boesemani and M. lacustris. (Photo: M. & C. Piednoir)

Telmatherinidae

The members of this family – with one exception – are endemic to the Indonesian island Celebes (Sulawesi). Most of the members of the family belong to the genus *Telmatherina*. They chiefly inhabit the soft water and slightly acidic standing waters. There the adult fishes seem to prefer the open water, while the water parts with dense vegetation are chiefly visited for spawning purposes.

Basically the maintainence of rainbowfishes and blue-eyes in the aquarium is identical to that of all other fish species. That is the reason for me to refer to the many basic aquarium books on the market and thus to concentrate on information which is important for rainbowfishes.

The aquarium

Each of the usually offered aquaria is suitable for the keeping of rainbowfishes or other atherinid fishes. However, as many of these fishes really like to swim in the open water the aquarium may be too small but practically never can be too large. As a general rule for the aquarium community one can say:

1 cm adult fish = 1 litre water.

It's important to pronounce the suffix "adult" before "fish", because that's what has to be taken into consideration from the beginning. That means, that ten specimens of the Chequered Rainbowfish, *Melanotaenia splendida inornata*, which can reach a length of up to 15 cm, have to

A male Melanotaenia splendida inornata from Flat Rock Creek, Arnhem Land. Today we can't understand why the first describer, Castelnau, named this fish inornata (= inornate). (Photo: G. Schmida)

be kept in an aquarium which at least contains 150 l (40 gallons) of water.

The right place

As with all other aquaria, a rainbowfish aquarium shouldn't have direct sunlight for a too long time. However, whoever finds a place for his rainbowfish aquarium where it doesn't get at least one or two hours direct sunlight in the morning hours misses one of the greatest pleasures in rainbowfish keeping, the wonderful mating display in the morning hours which starts with the first sun beams. Nearly all rainbowfishes show their brightest colours and their most colourful mating display in the early morning hours.

Lighting and bottom

As with other fish, rainbowfish aquaria should have intensive lighting. The aim is to find the best way between good plant growth and algae growth. Normally ten to twelve hours are enough, some experimentation may be helpful.
The bottom should consist of dark gravel with a diameter between 4 and 6 mm. The dark colour of the gravel intensifies the colours of the rainbowfishes.

The planting

Unfortunately there aren't many plants in the commercial trade from the natural habitats of the rainbowfishes and atherinid fishes. The Madagascan Aponogeton *(Aponogeton madagascariensis)* is one of the few exceptions. However, normally all plants are suitable which do well with the light offered.
Most of all it is important to have plants. As mentioned before, this is not the case in all of the natural biotopes. However, there are good reasons to use natural water plants. Beside the aestethic impression for the viewer they are important for the water care. With strong lighting the plants produce oxygen during day times. They additionally remove the ammonium and nitrate ions from the water, the latter being produced at the end of the nitrogen decomposing processes, as these are plant nutrients. Additionally, they help to stabilize the pH value most of all in softer water. Last but not least they make good hiding places for non-dominant fishes and are a good spawning substrate. However, they mustn't grow too densely as then they might leave too few free swimming place

for the fishes, and the photosynthesis may lead to a too strong increase of the pH value.
To make a plant suitable as a spawning substrate it just needs to be rather fineleaved or have some thinner parts. The swimming roots of *Heteranthera zosterifolia* are as suitable as is Java moss *(Vesicularia dubyana)*. The latter one additionally tolerates a certain amount of salt added to the water, but for some species (blueeyes) which have to be kept in seawater of at least 20 ‰ salt (seawater normally has 35‰) you may also take sea algae.

Filter and aeration

Because of the strong metabolism of most rainbowfishes good filters are necessary. The total volume of the aquarium should be circulated at least three times an hour. At the filter outlet you should fix a diffuser to guarantee a good oxygen supply. Not only the fishes but also the plants (in not very well lighted aquaria also during the day hours!) consume oxygen as does the nitrate reducing processes in the filter. If your aquarium is densely planted or if you have too many fishes in your aquarium, you will need an additional air supply from an electric air pump and an airstone.

Heating

Although the rainbowfishes and most of their relatives are typical tropical fishes most of them are kept too warm. A temperature between 22 and 24°C (72 and 75°F) is totally satisfactory for nearly all species. Quite on the contrary, higher temperatures seem to lead to a higher susceptibility to certain diseases (see there). Also for breeding you don't have to increase temperature. The species originating from the Australian south or from the higher parts of New Guinea will easily tolerate temperatures down to 18°C (64°F), for a period of several weeks. Most of them even don't reduce spawning with these temperatures. However, in any case temperature changes should be gradual as many species seem to be sensitive to sudden temperature changes. That has also to be remembered when doing water changes.

More decorations

Driftwood should only be used for species which need slightly acidic water. In all other species it is undesired and may even be harmful. Hidingplaces built from stones may be used in any case, but for safety reasons they should be spliced together with silicone. Too many decorations will prevent the easy catching of the fish which may be necessary from time to time.

Tap water is first choice

The rule for most of the rainbowfishes is: the best water is coming directly from the tap. This water normally is medium hard to hard with a hardness of more than 10°dGH (180 ppm). Only if you have chloramine in your water do you have to use a good chloramine remover. Although most of the rainbowfishes come from slightly acidic and soft water, it is easier to keep them in harder water, for several reasons.

It has already been stated that rainbowfishes seem to be a rather young family which originates from seawater. This is the reason why many of them show a high tolerance of harder water (although an addition of salt normally isn't helpful at all). But more importantly, harder water doesn't show as many and as sudden changes in the pH value as soft water may show. And these changes – which do not occur in nature – are not loved by many rainbowfishes as for most other aquarium fishes.

However, you can also use tap water if it is softer than 10°dGH (180 ppm). But then you need more regular water changes (see below). Only a few rainbowfishes really need hard or soft water. As mentioned, *Melanotaenia trifasciata* from the Goyder River needs harder water than all the other forms of that species, while contrary *M. praecox* needs soft water. *Bedotia* and *Marosatherina* may be kept like the other rainbowfishes, while the blue-eyes usually need hard water with a slight addition of salt, according to their origin.

Nitrites and nitrates

In the aquarium, the waste products of fishes undergo the so-called nitrogen cycle. Consequently, bacteria are needed which aren't present in newly established aquaria. Until then, the reduction of the waste products rests at the stage where the nitrite ions are poisonous for fishes even in small amounts (for some species at less than 0. 2 mg/l). If you decorate an aquarium for the first time, you shouldn't add any fish for three weeks. To accelerate the cycling processes you may add some filter mass (or gravel) from a long running aquarium (do not transport it for more than a few minutes as otherwise all bacteria

will die from a lack of oxygen) or you may also use a starter culture available in some petshops. Then you can add fish after one week. If the aquarium has too high a nitrite level, the fish will hover directly under the surface and breathe heavily despite seemingly adequate filtration and additional aeration.

The final product of the nitrogen reducing processes are nitrate ions. These aren't poisonous to fish in normal concentrations. They are reduced by the uptake of the plants and by regular water changes.

above: Howard Swamps southeast of Darwin near Howard Springs in the Northern Territory, habitat of Pseudomugil tenellus and Melanotaenia nigrans below: Roper River near Mataranka, N.T., habitat of Melanotaenia splendida australis. (Photos: N. Grunwald)

Water changes

A regular water change is necessary under all circumstances. In nature nearly all atherinform fishes live in clear, fresh water. If you make a 20% water change of the same temperature about every two weeks the fishes will thank you with brighter colours and more active behaviour.

THE RIGHT FOOD

Rainbowfishes are omnivorous. There are few kinds of food they will not eat voraciously. This is similar to their larger relatives. Although they have a comparatively large mouth, they normally have a rather narrow throat. Therefore, the foods must not be too large.

The blue eyes and threadfin rainbowfish *Iriatherina werneri* are an exception to the rule. They will be discussed separately.

Flake food

A commercial fish food – either flake or granulated – may be the basic diet for all rain-bowfish species. To guarantee that the vitamins added to most of the food offered today are still available, the food should not be purchased later than four months after the production date. Additionally all food should be consumed quickly once the package has been opened. Therefore, smaller portions should be purchased more frequently than buying larger food containers although these may be cheaper. Tablet food is not useful since it generally is ignored once it has sunk to the bottom. It is important to feed only as much as is eaten within about 15 minutes.

Live food

Unfortunately it has become more difficult to catch live food on your own. Nutrient rich settling tanks of sewage purification plants have become rare, as most of the contemporary facilities have installed a third, phosphate reducing plant. Many other ponds are protected by law as the last refuges for our threatened amphibians, reptiles and rare water insects. But wherever it's still possible, aquarists should take advantage of the opportuniy to catch their own live food and try to supply their fish with pond food at least from time to time.

Occasionally the commercial trade offers bloodworms or red mosquito larvae, glass worms or white mosquito larvae, brine shrimps, daphniae and tubifex. These may be offered as tidbits to most larger rainbows.

Most of all brine shrimp naupliae can be hatched at home. The dry eggs (be careful to avoid purchasing eggs that are too old and not stored in a frost free freezer) are added to a salt solution (10–20‰) and with sufficient aeration hatched within one or two days. They are then ready to be fed. Once accustomed to them, even large rainbowfishes relish them. They are a nearly ideal food.

In nature, several species take some of their food, such as ants, from the surface. A somewhat easier way to supply foods (also some ants are protected by law) is the raising of fruit flies *(Drosophila)*. To avoid a fly invasion, you should always use the wingless variety (and make sure that culture openings are inaccessible to wild flies). Starter cultures may be obtained from other aquarists or from the specialized trade. Culture manuals can also be purchased from supply houses.

It is also easy to breed whiteworms or the smaller grindal worms. However, they should be fed to rainbowfishes no more often than once a week because of their high fat content.

Frozen food

The pet trade offers a large variety of frozen foods, most of all bloodworms in Europe and brine shrimp in North America. However, persons suffering from an allergy have to be very careful with bloodworms because the hemoglobin included (even more dangerous in freeze dried bloodworms) may cause very serious skin and respiratory duct irritations. However, all other suitably sized frozen foods are suitable. One must not defrost the frozen food before adding it to the water but present it to the fish in modest portions. In contrast to the current opinion among many aquarists, this reduces the pollutants which quickly develop during the defrosting. Fish can't get a stomach cold. But all decomposing food worsens the water quality significantly.

Plant food

As omnivorous species, most of the larger rainbows are also interested in plant food. Actually they don't harm the water plants but the larger species seem to have a preference for the normally unpopular water lenses or duckweeds *(Lemna)*. Flake foods produced on a plant base

General Maintainance
The Proper Diet

may also be recommended. Freshly hatched fry may also benefit from the so-called green water which is clouded by microscopically small algae. To produce them you just have to expose used aquarium water (in the summer) into the open light (or indoors under a 24 hour light), and after one or two weeks, the algae (and protozoans) will have developed.

Additional fry food

For most of the smaller fry of the melanotaeniid species (see under breeding), a special food is needed. Besides the rotatoriae (rotifers) and infusoriae (protists), the smallest flake (and powdered) foods have proved suitable. Ready-to-use food – the food offered in the normal pet-shops normally is too large – may be purchased from the commercial fish suppliers. Also APR, a special fry food not available everywhere, is useful. But you also can easily and successfully produce your own fine flake food, e. g. with the help of an old coffee mill or a mortar. You may also add cooked, dried and powdered egg yolks.
Young blue-eyes may be fed with newly hatched brine shrimp naupliae directly after birth, other rainbowfishes after two or three weeks. But as unhatched eggs (and shells) may constipate the digestive duct if consumed, care must be taken to separate naupliae and eggs. Therefore, stop the aeration in the breeding container before harvesting. The eggs shells migrate to the surface, some unhatched eggs and undissolved salt sink to the bottom. With a little tube (or baster) you now can draw off nearly pure naupliae. The rest, when rinsed, can be fed to the larger fish who aren't harmed by a few egg shells or unhatched eggs which pass harmlessly through the digestive tract.
I often feed brine shrimp naupliae. In a bottle with a content of about one and a half liter (ca. 0.4 gals) it is possible to hatch about 20 ml of dry eggs. My own experiences show that the eggs I use – which normally come from the Salt Lake in Utah, USA) – show a better hatching rate if I use less salt, about 10 g/l.
At the same time that newly hatched brine shrimp naupliae are accepted the fry also take microworms. These can easily be raised. Additionally the fry accept vinegar eels. The latter can also be bred by oneself. However, the cleaning and separation of them from the vinegar before feeding is a little bit more time consuming. These two food varieties are also available from other aquarists or from the trade,

along with culturing instructions. Any food changes have to be made very carefully. There have been many cases where all the youngsters died because of too radical a food change within a short time.

Food frequency

Fry may be fed up to six times a day, but only with the smallest portions. With growth this should decrease. Adult fishes shouldn't be fed more than once a day, with one fasting day per week. During a vacation, the older ones can be left without food for as long as two weeks. Many more fishes have been killed by too much food fed by well meaning "fishsitters" than starved during an absence of a few days.
Working people normally can't feed their fry as often. However, inventive aquarists have built small apparatusses using a digital timer, an electric air pump, a small bottle or glass (filled with some powder flake food) with lid and some tubes. A tube is installed between the pump through the tightly closed lid nearly to the bottom of the bottle and another one through the lid to the fry tank. Now you program the air pump in such a way that it is set to work every four hours for exactly one minute (that's why you need a digital timer). This way the fish are fed even if you are not home.

Food for blue-eyes
and *Iriatherina werneri*

The smaller relatives of the atherinids do not really like flake food. Most of all, if you want higher numbers of eggs, a larger part of the diet should consist of small live food. Anyone who doesn't have a pond food supply should feed baby brine shrimp at least twice a week. Microworms likewise are very suitable for these fish which rarely grow larger than 4 cm.
Those Blue-eyes, which have to be kept in water with salt added, will find brine shrimp naupliae especially suitable since the shrimp stay alive, even in brackish water, for at least two days. Of course this has a very positive effect on fry growth.

Food for other atherinid fishes

All other atheriniform fishes offered in the trade, Bedotiidae and Telmatherinidae, may be fed like the rainbowfishes. For the comfortable acclimatization of new fishes you may especially

Reproduction
Breeding Preparations

Two impressing males of Iriatherina werneri. (Photo: R. Kuiter)

feed brine shrimp naupliae. *Telmatherina* species should get these on a regular base.

One point discussed before: The species community

Rainbowfishes are swarm fishes. You should never purchase a school of less than six or better yet, ten specimens. So you already need a relatively large aquarium for a single species. More will be needed for a community of fishes.

As already mentioned, rainbowfishes may be associated with nearly all other peaceful aquarium fishes. Most of all, bottom dwelling fishes are recommended since they make excellent companions as scavengers for remaining food. Additionally, nearly all of the larger rainbowfishes may be associated with each other and with their atheriniform relatives. However, if you want to breed a species then you must not associate similarly species with each

other. It is not useful to keep more than one colour variety of a species as the females resemble one another. The same is true with nearly all *Chilatherina* females. Also the smaller rainbowfishes and the blue-eyes are slower feeders and should be kept in quarters especially for themselves.

Sex differences

The sexes are not always easy to distinguish in rainbowfishes. Generally, the males have a more elongated first and a second dorsal fin which at least reaches to the caudal fin. But this elongation of the dorsal and anal fins may often not be seen before the fishes are adult. Another difference is that the colours of the males are nearly always more prominent. Additionally, the males of nearly all melanotaeniid fishes show another special feature. During the mating and impressing behaviour, the males show a mating stripe which reaches from the tip of the snout to at least the base of the first dorsal fin. This mating stripe may be yellow, golden, brown or even light blue. The pigment cells responsible for the forming of the stripe may be extended within parts of seconds as well as contracted again, with the result, that the mating stripe may be switched on and off like a traffic light. In fresh water even semi-adult males show this stripe. If you place a swarm of semi-adult rainbowfishes in a bucket with slightly cooler fresh water, you often can distinguish the males easily by looking from the top as they already show their mating stripe. Only the rainbowfishes of the *Melanotaenia splendida* relatives don't show the mating stripe.

Unfortunately the atherinid fishes like *Cratero-cephalus* are very difficult to sex. So you have to buy at least six, better ten specimens. In this case the odds of having purchased both sexes is high.

left: The Neon Rainbowfish Melanotaenia praecox belongs to the most bred species. (Photo: H.-G. Evers)

right: To spawn (here M. boesemani) the male lures the female to the spawning substrate and factually pushes it into it. (Photo: U. Werner)

Reproduction
Breeding Preparations

Crosses

Possibly because of their relatively young evolutionary history and their close genetic relationship, many of the rainbowfishes may be crossed with each other. That is relevant for nearly all melanotaeniids, but also the bedotiids and telmatherinids. Not only can species within a family cross, but even species from different families have been known to cross. And it is not true that the fishes don't cross if they can find partners of their own kind in the same aquarium, this seems to be not important since they will spawn with a number of partners. On the other hand, hybrids are very rare in nature, although up to four different rainbowfish species may be found in one habitat.

As far as known blue-eyes haven't been crossed yet – intentionally or by chance – in the aquarium. Neither are natural hybrids known. Nothing is available concerning the possibility of crossing atherinid fishes.

Fry which grow up in the community aquarium must not be given to other keepers. Additionally, you have to use separate breeding aquaria for every species or variety. Several of the crosses are not fertile, but some will reproduce normally. Unfortunately, crosses sometimes show up in the commercial trade.

Fishes with the pseudoscientific names *"Melanotaenia hammeri"*, *"M. marci"* and *"M. greeti"* are crosses which should neither be offered nor purchased. The species found in nature make a better looking exhibit anyway. The so-called new species are a fraud foisted upon unknowing rainbowfish enthusiasts, as those animals are counterfeited in the search for new species and products.

This Bedotia species was dealt with as B. geayi until recently. However, it probably represents another species, B. madagascariensis. More details in the AQUALOG-Lexicon. (Photo: H. Hieronimus)

left: Two day old fry of Glossolepis incisus.

right: Eggs of Melanotaenia praecox. The white egg was unfertilized and got fungus. (Photos: M. & C. Piednoir)

Reproduction
The Breeding

The breeding aquarium

The simplest way to breed rainbowfish is to set up of a special breeding aquarium. The decoration of this aquarium may be modest. All that is needed is some aeration, aged tap water, a hiding place for non-dominant specimens, and a spawning mop or plant bush. No filter is necessary. All atherinid fishes show one peculiarity; they are permanent spawners. That means that they may lay eggs on an almost daily basis during their reproductively active time, which starts when the fishes are semi-adult and may last until a considerable age. Even twelve year old females of *Melanotaenia trifasciata* have laid eggs which developed into normal fry after insemination. Freshly wild caught specimens, placed into a small photo tank directly after capture, have started spawning, as have fish which were bought in a shop and set into an aquarium with fresh water only hours later at home.

There may be phases when no eggs are spawned. However, the egg release may be stimulated when the fish are kept some time without water changes, but with sufficient feeding. A large water change after some weeks will initiate the spawning spontaneously in most cases. If you want to produce more eggs at one time, you may also separate the partners for one week before you place them into the spawning tank.

The eggs

As already mentioned, the eggs are released daily. They have a hard shell and little sticky filaments with which they adhere to the plants or any artificial spawning medium. Taken between the fingers, you can feel the eggs easily. If they burst while rolled between the fingers, they weren't fertilized. The eggs of the rainbowfishes have a diameter of about 1 mm, eggs of blue-eyes are appreciably larger, nearly 2 mm. The time the eggs need until they hatch varies, but in part depends upon temperature. At a temperature of 24°C (75°F) the rainbowfish fry hatch after six to seven days, while the eggs of the blue-eyes will need 14 to 18 days under those conditions.

The lengthy incubation time is the reason why you can leave the eggs for some days with the parents. Many rainbowfishes, however, try to search out and eat some of the spawn. But if you use a suitable spawning substrate – Java moss or synthetic yarn mops have been proved to be best

– you can avoid this to a large degree, as the rainbowfishes normally don't lay the eggs directly on the surface of the substrate.

The spawning substrate

As already mentioned, bushes of Java moss or other fineleaved plants do well as spawning substrates. They may be placed at any spot in the aquarium but should be at least as large as a fist. Spawning mops may be produced by yourself. Therefore roll synthetic yarn over a 20 to 25 cm board or book which has been wrapped with a piece of thick paper. Natural fibers have not stood up to the test and may become rotten and pollute the water. As soon as you have rolled about 30 to 40 layers of yarn around the paper, remove the yarn carefully. The upper edge of the bundle is now carefully tied together, drawn over a cork, an empty film cannister or another float and then bound together tightly beneath it. The yarn is finally cut at the lower edge and the spawning mop is ready to use.

The colour of the fibers does not seem to be important. However, dark colours have proved to be best if one wants to pick eggs (see below) as the eggs are more easily recognized.

The spawning

The male initiates the spawning sequence by trying to attract the female. Hence it often displays his body in front of the female, presenting its forehead. In the species which have a mating stripe, (see p. 20) it starts lighting or "flashing" at that point. If the female seems to be interested, i. e. if she doesn't swim away, the male becomes more obtrusive and tries to lure the female to a suitable spawning site. At the same time, it presents its flanks and shows its brightest and most intensive colours. If the female isn't attracted by the male's overatures, males of most of the larger species may become somewhat more aggressive and will try to violently push the female to the spawning substrate. Therefore, every spawning aquarium – as well as every community aquarium or the normal maintenance aquarium, as these are also used continously for spawning purposes – should consist of more hiding-places then there are females in the aquarium to give them a chance to hide from overly amorous males.

Fish which are in a spawning aquarium have to be observed carefully. If the female seems to be threatened, the partners have to be separated.

Reproduction
The Breeding

Therefore it is often useful to keep two females with a male for spawning.

If the fish are close to the spawning substrate, the male pushes the female to the surface of the substrate with its own body. If both partners are nearly in the same position and tight to the spawning location, the fish really shoot away from the substrate.

If Java moss or articificial spawning mops are used, the eggs are nearly injected into them and thus most are safe from their hungry parents, that extra female and any other rainbowfishes of the same species present. (Of course they are all of the same species to avoid crosses.)

Essentially the spawning in the blue-eyes is very similar. With spread fins, the male tries to entice the female to the spawning substrate. Once there the blue-eye male also pushes the female into the spawning substrate surface and the fishes again shoot away after the egg and sperm release. Blue-eyes and rainbowfishes don't have a certain preference for any water level while spawning. It is more important for them to find the suitable substrate even if it e. g. lays on the bottom of the tank.

The further treatment of the eggs

There are two basic ways to proceed after the spawning. First the parents may be placed back into their original aquarium after about seven days. Or, alternatively, the eggs can be removed from the tank. Therefore either exchange the spawning substrate for a new one or pick the eggs from the substrate. Doing this one needs not be afraid of damaging them. Fertilized eggs are rather hard. You just put them into a small tank with some aeration and add some methylene blue to prevent unfertilized eggs from getting fungus and maybe infecting the good ones. If all the eggs seem to be unfertilized either two females have spawned together (also this may happen occasionally) or you most possibly have a cross.

The fertilized eggs are extremely resistant to external influences. Cases exist where they survived the extensive rinsing of the substrate with ice cold water or even the desinfection of plants with alum. Therefore the substrate can be rinsed without problems using water of a moderate temperature before they are placed into the aquarium where the fry shall hatch. This reduces the possibility of waste material or other pollutants adhering to the eggs. Picking the eggs has only proved to be useful with smaller fish species, since the larger ones may produce up to 1,000 eggs within only a week. It is much more work to pick the eggs of larger rainbows from the substrate than to remove the substrate and replace it with a new one.

It is even possible to transport the eggs in wet substrate, e. g. wet Java moss or mops. From plants which have formerly been in a rainbowfish tank new breeding stocks have been started already several times (but be careful with crosses by transferring eggs from a community aquarium where several species are kept in). Plants suspected of carrying unwanted eggs can be quarantined themselves or placed in an aquarium without rainbows for some weeks until the suspect fry have hatched out.

The newly emerged rainbowfishes are very small and may be fed with the foods mentioned. Young blue-eyes are noticeably larger and may be fed with newly hatched brine shrimp naupliae from the start.

However, newly hatched fish don't need to be fed before 24 hours have passed as for this time they are still being nourished by the remainder of their yolk sac.

Alternative breeding methods

There are several more methods to be used if you only want to raise small numbers. The first may be used with smaller rainbowfishes and has to be tested to see if it works in your aquarium or not. The young fish are placed in their own aquarium before they have reached maturity. They must not be removed or placed into another aquarium. They start to spawn rather early under these circumstances. The plan is that they will get used to the fry which are relatively large for them in the beginning. The fry may be "accepted" as part of their environment. You should obtain not only enough fry to keep your own stock running but also to supply some of your friends with youngsters from time to time. Once working, this method will also function as the parent fish grow into later adulthood. However, if the parents are placed into another tank even for a few days, this method will stop.

With blue-eyes and also with some of the smaller rainbowfishes you may also cover a part of the water surface densely with floating plants. Between these you will always find a few fry which may grow up in the aquarium or, for a more professional raising, may be taken out with a spoon (or cup) and transferred into a rearing tank on their own.

Reproduction
The Breeding

Male Forktail Blue-eye, Pseudomugil furcatus, in mating colouration. (Photo: N. Armstrong)

A third method generally may be used with all of the fishes mentioned. It is based upon the fact that all of the newly hatched fry of the atherinid fishes stay directly under the water surface. Therefore, you separate a fifth of the aquarium – which may also be the normal species aquarium for permanent keeping – by a net or a screen wire in a way that is secured so that no larger fish can pass. Be careful that the screen wire is small enough that the adults can't catch their gills in it.

Close to the surface, the net openings should be a little larger to give the fry a chance to pass more easily. A commercial foam filter should be placed into the smaller partition and set so that the water outlet flows into the large partition. Several fry will swim into the smaller partition and stay as long as they are large enough that the spawners can't inhale them. Then they can be sold or placed into a grow out tank or to their parents.

Melanotaenia herbertaxelrodi, the Lake Tebera Rainbowfish. (Photo: G. Schmida)

Reproduction
Raising the Fry

Pair of the Burster Creek Rainbowfish, Melanotaenia trifasciata. The less colourful female is on the top.
(Photo: G. Maebe)

By the way, all the other atherinid fishes kept in aquaria may be bred in the same ways as the rainbowfishes.

The mailing of eggs

The relatively long time the incubating eggs need before hatching in combination with their resistance to temperature changes have led to the fact that rainbowfish friends all over the world trade eggs. The method has been developed originally by the Australian Ron BOWMAN, who sent several rainbowfish species to Europe this way. One should take the freshly spawned rainbowfish eggs (not older than 24 hours) or blue-eyes (not older than 4 days) and attach them to strands of synthetic yarn not longer than 3 cm. They should be placed as far away from each other as possible. Not more than 10 strands should be used. Those are then placed

Pair of Glossolepis spec. "Lake Kli" from the Mamberamo River area, the female in the background may be recognized by its shorter fins.
(Photo: G. Schmida)

into a small container (e. g. film or medicine – well rinsed! – cannisters) which are half filled with fresh water. One or more of the containers are then placed into a larger styrofoam container and then put into an upholstered envelope. To avoid large temperature changes, you may add a cannister with fat (e. g. butter). The envelopes are sent by airmail and will have about five days time to reach the addressee – enough to reach many countries.

Brackish water species

Especially among the blue-eyes *(Pseudomugil)* there are a few species which live in brackish or even in pure seawater. Among these are certain populations of *Pseudomugil cyanodorsalis* and *P. signifer.* To keep these fish prospering the right conditions already have to be established before the purchase of the fish. A suitable aquarium will need a few days for the salt to dissolve totally.

The specialty with these species is that they don't have to be kept in brackish water for their whole life but may also live in freshwater or seawater permanently after accomodation. However, as far as we know until today there are varieties originating from water with a larger salt content which have larger fins. In many cases those larger fins will not be that developed under freshwater conditions. For instance we know that certain especially longfinned varieties of the Pacific Blue-eye, *P. signifer,* will breed in freshwater without problems, however, the long fins won't develop in the offspring. They just get the "normal", short fins. However, in contrast you may also find long-finned varieties in pure freshwater like the fishes shown on p. 11, which came from Harvey Creek.

For these reasons it is extraordinarily important to know the origin of the fishes and as many details as is possible. Responsible breeders give away their fish only with such detailed instructions. The fry if at all possible, should be kept as they live under natural conditions, i. e. with a salt addition if originating from salt containing waters. This has the additional advantage that the brine shrimp naupliae live longer and the fry really "stay in the food".

Diet change

One of the most critical decisions when raising the fry is when to change the diet. Often there have been large losses of fry which normally were big enough to eat brine shrimp naupliae and, accordingly, got them. It often emerged afterwards that they had starved to death because they hadn't become used to the new food. Therefore, it appears that every diet change has to be introduced slowly – for a period of at least two weeks the old and new food should be fed together. No radical changes should be made.

Growth

If you want to breed rainbowfish or just want to raise the fry you must be very patient. Only a few species can be termed "fast growing". With nearly all larger rainbowfish it is necessary to wait at least one year until the fish are fully grown adults. However, even then they still keep on growing – very slowly. Rainbowfish kept in aquaria – in good conditions– tend to grow larger than they would in nature (e. g. *Melanotaenia boesemani* will grow to more than 20 cm) and, additionally, will become much older. One of the reasons is that they can obtain food on a regular base, a situation they aren't confronted with in nature regularly.

Only the smaller blue-eyes may be mature after about three months, with the best of diets and frequent water changes. But most rainbowfish and the other atheriniforms seem to need at least six months before they are mature. Grown to their normal full length, most species are one or one and a half years old. Unfortunately, most species don't show their brightest colours before that date.

Different fry length

By the continuous egg picking and the transfer of the fry into a grow-out tank it often happens that you gather a lot of fry with striking length differences. In this case, you have to provide sufficient numbers of hidingplaces (mostly plants) as the fry may be somewhat cannibalistic towards each other. A young fish of 2 cm may already eat a newborn fry. However, this is mainly relevant for the larger species.

Raise several species at one time

For rationalization reasons, several breeders try to raise the fry in a community grow-out tank. However, you can't do this if you can't easily tell the species apart, even if the fish are half grown. Thus it is no problem to combine and raise together young Boeseman's Rainbowfish *(M. boesemani)* and Lake Kutubu Rainbowfish *(M. lacustris),* but you must not put two

Diseases
The Quarantine-Aquarium

Chilatherina species in one raising tank as it may not even be possible to distinguish the females when they are adults.

Rainbowfish belong to the kind of aquarium fish which basically aren't easily susceptible to aquarium fish diseases. However, there are a few diseases which may be found in rainbowfish somewhat more frequently than others and are discussed below.

The basic rule is: prevention is better than treatment. Many diseases, and almost all bacterial infections (see page 29), are caused by so-called "weakness parasites". That means that the fish are only infected if they are affected by something else already. That may be permanent overfeeding or neglected water parameters (e. g. if you don't make regular water changes). Sudden environmental changes have proven to be especially detrimental. Although many rainbowfish are exposed to large temperature differences in nature due to seasonal changes, in the aquarium they show a greater sensitivity to bacterial infections if the temperature suddenly changes widely.

The quarantine aquarium

Before adding some new fish to one's stock, it is always a good practice to keep the fish in a special quarantine aquarium for some time. But by doing so, you already can make most of the possible mistakes.

The aquarium has to be sufficiently large to avoid unnecessary stress to the fish. For larger rainbowfish the volume has to be 100 liters or even more. To give the fish a secure feeling you should paint the back pane, the bottom and also the two side panes with a dark colour (from the outside) or stick dark cardboard to them. For the substrate you shouldn't use any gravel as infectious germs may survive there longer. Beside some slight aeration and – if necessary – a heater, you should provide some hiding places (for non-dominant fishes) and add some plastic plants. In no way should the aquarium be without decoration. You should use plastic plants as you can easily desinfect them, e. g. with alum. You don't need a filter as you should change about 15% of the water every three days with tempered fresh tap water (incl. removing all debris). Important: All setup and auxiliary materials may be used only for this aquarium and – if necessary – have to be desinfected after use.

It goes without saying that the fish, as long as they stay within this aquarium, have to be ob-

served at least twice a day and be fed at least once. The aquarium should always be ready to use even if you don't plan to purchase new fish. On the one hand, it enables you to buy fish spontaneously which would be impossible otherwise, and, on the other, you have always an aquarium at hand if you need one to treat a few fish from a community aquarium.

After a quarantine period without illness of about 14 days (or 14 days after a successful treatment) the aquarium is desinfected. Of course, there must not be any fish or plants left in the aquarium. To desinfect the aquarium you may use a chlorine bleach (bought in stores specializing in swimming pool equipment – but be careful, it's strongly caustic), hydrogen peroxide (H_2O_2, 6%, also caustic, be especially careful with the 30% solution, this is very caustic) or potassium permangante ($KMnO_4$, difficult to obtain by private persons in some countries) may be used. The chlorine bleach is used according to the instructions, hydrogen peroxide is added as follows: 250 ml/100 l (6%) or 50 ml/100 l (30% – do not make a mistake!). With the potassium permangante (be careful, it stains fingers and clothing very strongly!) you first prepare a basic solution (about 5 g/l). For desinfection purposes you carefully and slowly add as much of the solution until the water is opaque. The solutions remain in the aquarium for three days. In all cases you have to rinse out the aquarium carefully and then soak it for some more days before you change the water completely. Aquarium plants may be desinfected with potassium alum ($K_2SO_4 \cdot Al_2(SO4) \cdot 24\ H_2O$, poisonous if eaten!), by dissolving 10 g alum in 1 l water and soaking the plants in this solution for five minutes, rinse carefully afterwards.

A simpler method to desinfect the aquarium is with saltwater, mostly suitable for smaller aquaria and equipment. You dissolve 35 g salt (it may be the cheapest from the super market) per liter water. According to UNTERGASSER, you may also spread a salt paste onto the panes (just add enough water to the salt until you have a paste) and clean the aquarium after the paste has dried up. But now to the most important diseases.

Whitespot disease

One of the most frequent diseases in aquarium fish (and therefore in atheriniform fish) and, at the same time, one of the most easily cured diseases, is the whitespot disease. The infection by the ciliates (large protozoa) *Ichthyophthirius*

Diagnosis and Treatment

In healthy fish the scale rows are very symmetric, the fins are complete, as seen here in a wild-caught male of the Lake Kutubu Rainbowfish, Melanotaenia lacustris. (Photo: G. R. Allen)

multifiliis, also known as Ichthyophtiriasis or more easily Ich can easily be recognized by the presence of small white spheric balls of about 1 mm diameter, which normally first appear on the fins, later on the body as well, and finally cover the whole body of the fish. Infected fish do not behave normally, they swim lethargically and scratch themselves from time to time on the decorations. Not treated, the infection leads to the death of the fish within days or weeks.

The cure of the whitespot disease can be achieved only indirectly. The ciliates grow to a diameter of about 1.5 mm and have the form of white little balls. To reproduce they leave their host (i. e. the fish) and divide themselves, with the result that up to more than 1,000 microscopically small swarmers emerge, which at once start the search for a new host fish – where they can grow. If densely covering the fish, the white spots weaken the fish and cause its death. You can only kill the swarmers. There are three basic ways to do this:

1. Heat treatment: The aquarium is heated up to 30°C (86°F), better 32°C (90°F). This temperature is not tolerated by the swarmers. But since rainbowfish are sensitive to sudden temperature increases this method can only partially be recommended.

Blue-eyes, like this wildcaught male Pseudomugil connieae from the vicinity of Popondetta, Papua New Guinea, are not very sensitive to diseases. (Photo: N. Armstrong)

2. Water treatment: The commercial trade offers several suitable medications, most of them based on malachite green oxalate. This method kills the swarmers in the water, therefore the treatment can be stopped two days after you haven't noticed any more white spots on the fish.

3. Medical food: The feeding of a specially medicated food prohibits the reinfection of the fish with the swarmers. The – exclusive – feeding with this food must be continued for at least three weeks.

For the time of the treatment the fish must not be placed in another aquarium as *Ichthyophthirius multifiliis* may form stages which encapsulate and are present latently. This is the reason, why, e. g. after a water change in an aquarium, where no new fish have been introduced for long time, Ich may occur. Therefore, you always should have an emergency supply of this medications on hand, especially for weekends.

Velvet disease

Fish infected with a flagellate – in most cases it is *Oodinium pillularis* – look like as if they are powdered with fine spots. Looking against the light, the skin looks like velvet. In rare cases, only the gills are infected, and the fish breath quite heavily (this kind of infection may be mistaken for a nitrite poisoning, see page 30). The petshops offer some really helpful remedies to treat this infection, most of them base on methylene blue or copper sulphate.

Ulcers

Rainbowfish seem to be infected with ulcers more often than other fish. This may have three different bacterial causes. Nevertheless, all of them have in common that they are "weakness parasites" which only occur when the keeping conditions are not at an optimum. Many ulcers seem to be caused by sudden environmental changes. Aquaria which are located in the house where they heat up in the summer are potentially threatened as are aquaria where the normally regular water change is overdue for some time. A good preventive measure in these cases is to increase the temperature slowly at the beginning of the warm season. And, of course, regular water changes are a must.

If you see the first signs of an ulcer optimize the aquarium conditions and start treatment as

Diseases
Bacterial Infections

outlined. If fish are infected and you want to keep the stock, start breeding them at once. Fishes not yet seriously infected with ulcers normally still breed without problems and a transfer of the disease to the fry is rarely found.

With stronger infections and if the recommended treatment fails to be successful, the fish have to be euthanized. They are treated with a suitable narcotic added to the water. You may purchase these narcotics from your local veterinary.

BACTERIAL INFECTIONS

Fish which are permanently kept under temperature conditions of less than 24°C (75°F) seem to be less sensitive to bacterial infections than fish kept permanently in "high temperature aquaria". We often find the case that in a community aquarium only one species seems to be infected. Then, the fish may be cured as individuals in the quarantine aquarium (see above). Healthy fish are able to resist without problems a certain amount of causative agents present in every aquarium. The differentiation between the three different kinds of bacteria described in the following is not possible for the layman, even specialists have problems with the exact detection.

Aeromonas

The bacterial infection which perhaps occurs most frequently in the aquarium is Aeromonas. The most frequent representative of this genus is A. hydrophila, but other species may participate. If infected seriously, large ulcers appear which finally lead to the death of the fish. A treatment is only possibly with antibiotics (in most countries you need a prescription to purchase them), especially with Furazolidon (1 g/100 g food) or Aqua Furan® sometimes offered in good petshops. You may also try to cure the fish with Nitrofurantoin® (by ratiopharm), add one capsule to 40 l water.

Columnaris

This infection starts as initially small, whitish parts in the mouth area, the next step normally is that the fins ravel out and finally the body is infected. The first counteraction is an immediate improvement of the environmental conditions. Additionally you can try to treat the infection with acriflavine (trypaflavine). The remedy, available in drugstores, normally without

prescription may also be used as a preventative agent. The basic solution according to UNTERGASSER is 1 g/l water. For prevention purposes add 1 mg/l, for the treatment of already infected fish 3 mg/l (for slightly infected fish) to up to 5 ml/l. Acriflavine is also proven to be suitable to protect eggs against fungus.

Vibriosis

Less frequently, you may find an infection by representatives of the bacteria genus *Vibrio*, which has a similar manifestation. A treatment has little chances of success.

Fish tuberculosis

Fish tuberculosis is triggered by bacteria of the genus *Mycobacterium* and has a similar manifestation as *Aeromonas* or *Vibrio* infections. A successful treatment is nearly impossible.

On the use of antibiotics

Relatively often for the treatment of bacterial diseases like fish tuberculosis the use of antibiotics is recommended. However, this is questionable for several reasons:
First of all, the success of the treatment is very doubtful. In most cases the medication does not produce the expected results. Secondly, the

Male Yirrkala Rainbowfish, Melanotaenia trifasciata, with clearly visible ulcer.

In this female Melanotaenia trifasciata an ulcer nearly covers the complete caudal peduncle.
(Photos: G. Maebe)

uncontrolled use of antibiotics causes the development of antibiotic resistant bacteria strains which may not be cured with antibiotics even in an emergency. Thirdly, the latter is important as fish tuberculosis, although only in rare cases, may infect humans. And if the infection were caused by a strain which developed a resistance against certain antibiotics, the treatment becomes more difficult than expected.

The possible transfer of these bacteria to humans leads to the recommendation not to expose open wounds to aquarium water. If you notice small injuries which discharge matter and don't heal for a long time and if you had had contact with aquarium water, in very rare cases you might be infected with fish tuberculosis and should tell your doctor about your suspicion.

Intestinal parasites

Occasionally, rainbowfish and their relatives have transparent to whitish threadlike excrements. If they get thinner in spite of good feeding, you may most likely diagnose an infection with intestinal parasites (worms). A suitable treatment to cure the infection is the use of Concurat®-L (10%) or Droncit®, both in several countries prescription free medications produced by Bayer AG. The latter contains Praziquantel which is an especially well working ingredient which safely kills several kinds of worms.

Dosage: 2 g Concurat®-L are dissolved in 1 l water into which live bloodworms are added (be careful as these may cause allergies in aquarists). As soon as the first bloodworms die, you feed the rest to the fish. Or you can mix 500 mg Concurat®-L into 100 g of the normal food. Droncit®: Pulverize a quarter tablet and mix it into 100 g of the normal diet.

Tillerhead worms

The livebearing tillerhead worms of the species *Camallanus cotti* affect the rectum of the fish. Infected fish may be recognized by small worms hanging out of the intestine although you only see part of it. Heavily infected fish will get thinner and die. A good treatment success has been achieved with e. g. Flubendazol (Flubenol®5%, by Janssen) which may also be used against gill and skin worms. Dosage: 200 mg/100 l aquarium water. Other anthelmintic medicaments may have an effect also. As all of these medications need a prescription in many countries, you have

to contact a veterinary. In all cases the treatment has to be repeated three weeks after the first treatment.

Other diseases

If you are confronted with other diseases you should contact the specialized literature (see literature list on page 46).

Poisoning

Two kinds of poisoning which occur most often do not really belong to the diseases but shall, nevertheless, be dealt with in this column.

Nitrite poisoning

In newly set up aquaria, or in aquaria where the bacterial fauna has been destroyed by medications or aquaria which are overcrowded, the nitrogen cycle may be interrupted. If the nitrite level increases to more than 0.5 mg/l the fish hover directly under the water surface and breath heavily (attention, this may also be a oxygen deficiency – control your filter!). The only useful remedy is a larger water change with tempered fresh water which, in these circumstances, has to be repeated several times in one day, until the nitrite level is below 0. 2 mg/l at two successive measurements. Suitable test kits may be purchased in petshops (Check the expiry date!). The velvet disease may be mistaken with the nitrite poisoning (see page 28).

Acid and alkali diseases

If your aquarium is densely planted, the water change is overdue, the aquarium is overcrowded or if you use very soft rain or tap water, the pH value may increase or decrease strongly within a short period. The fish really shoot through the aquarium apparently haphazardly and sometimes even try to jump out of the water. If you make this observation, you have to make an immediate partial water change. If you know of one of the mentioned risc factors you have to measure the pH value weekly. Suitable tests are offered in the pet trade.

The Fishes
Rainbowfishes

Only a few of the more than 300 species of atheriniform fishes *(Atheriniformes)* known today (of which more than 100 species have been kept in the aquarium hobby at least once already) may be presented in this book. Nevertheless, some of the groups or species shall be mentioned below as the limited space permits:

Family Melanotaeniidae-Rainbowfish

Rainbowfish may be subdivided into a few different groups based on their bodyshape and their degree of relationship.

Melanotaenia splendida-group

The representatives of this group nearly all originate from Australia. The four Australian subspecies of the large growing species *Melanotaenia splendida* belong to this group as does the Crimson-Spotted Rainbowfish *(M. duboulayi)*, the Murray River Rainbowfish *(M. fluviatilis)* – the latter two species can practically only be distinguished by their larvae and possibly by their eggs – and the Lake Eacham Rainbowfish *(M. eachamensis)* and, additionally, some related but yet undescribed species from the Lake Eacham vicinity in Queensland (see also the chapter "Endangered species" in this book). From New Guinea, the Red-Striped Rainbowfish *M. splendida rubrostriata* and Parkinson's Rainbowfish, *M. parkinsoni,* are added.
These species in general are large, deepbodied species which attain a length of more than 10 cm, in many cases more than 14 cm. There is one exception: the Lake Eacham Rainbowfish and its relatives, whose taxonomic measures (fin ray counts, vertebrae, scales) are obviously smaller than in *M. splendida,* it is a socalled reduction species.

Melanotaenia nigrans-group

This group consists of especially elongated species which in nature may reach a length no longer than 10 cm. In addition to *M. nigrans, M. gracilis* and *M. exquisita* belong into this group. All of these species originate from the most extreme north of Australia. With the exception of one population of the Black-banded Rainbowfish *M. nigrans* they originate from an area west of the Gulf of Carpentaria.

Melanotaenia trifasciata-group

Although –scientifically speaking – this group consists of only a single species, it is justifiable to speak of a group. All varieties are large and in nature reach more than 10 cm in length. Not all of them are deepbodied, e. g. the variety from Goyder River stay more slender than most of the other representatives of the species (s. local varieties, p 38 ff), which are known from all over the north of Australia (most of all from the rivers which flow into the Gulf of Carpentaria).

Melanotaenia maccullochi-group

The group consists of rainbowfishes with a length of about 7 cm, only moderately deep-bodied, with only one species, the Dwarf Rainbowfish *Melanotaenia maccullochi,* occurring in Australia. All of the other species are known from Papua New Guinea. Among these species, the Fly River Rainbowfish *M. sexlineata,* and the Papua Rainbowfish *M. papuae* have to be mentioned, and, as the most recently described species, *M. caerulea.*
A colour variety of *M. splendida australis* was known under the name of *M. papuensis* which had been kept already for several years by aquarists. It is characterized by a prominent red lateral stripe and a dark posterior lower part of the body.
The real Papua Rainbowfish has been imported just recently and has been kept in aquaria for only short period of time (see poster).

Melanotaenia goldiei-group

Perhaps the species which originate from New Guinea are the closest relatives of the Australian *M. trifasciata.* Generally, these are large rainbow-fish which attain a length of 10 cm or more. However, only a few of them (e. g. *M. affinis*) are as deepbodied as these species and are more similar to the Goyder River variety. The rainbowfish from the great lakes belong into this group as well, e. g. *M. boesemani, M. lacustris* and *M. herbertaxelrodi.* The most widespread of these species is *M. affinis,* a species which may be easily recognized by its prominent white stripe below the dark lateral stripe and thus distinguished from the other species. Also the Mountain Rainbowfish, *M. monticola,* belongs into this group, and, with its origin from a heigth of 1,600 m, it is the rainbowfish which occurs at the highest elevation.

Two impressing males of the Wonga Creek Rainbowfish, Melanotaenia trifasciata. (Photo: G. Maebe)

Mating males of Melanotaenia cf. exquisita from Waterfall Creek. (Photo: G. Schmida)

lower left: Male Melanotaenia goldiei. (Photo: G. W. Lange)

lower right: Adult male Melanotaenia kamaka. (Photo: G. R. Allen)

Melanotaenia praecox-group

Although already caught and scientifically described in 1910, it may have been Dr. Gerald ALLEN who, in 1991, was the first to observe them with the view of an aquarist and recognized their beauty. But it was left to Heiko BLEHER to import these fish in 1992 for aquaristic purposes to

The Fishes
Rainbowfishes

Melanotaenia pierucciae, Pierrucia's Rainbowfish. (Photo: G. R. Allen)

Chilatherina bleheri, Bleher's Rainbowfish, wildcaught specimen from Danau Bira (Lake Holmes). (Photo: G. R. Allen)

lower left: Melanotaenia sp. „Batanta", from Batanta Island (may be identic with M. misoolensis). (Photo: N. Armstrong)

lower right: North New Guinea Rainbowfish, Melanotaenia affinis, from the Sepik River near Pagwi, PNG. (Photo: G. W. Lange)

Europe. This is a group of small (rarely more than 7 cm, in nature they tend to stay smaller, in the aquarium they may grow even larger) rainbowfish which become rather deepbodied when old.

As well as *M. praecox* also *M. kamaka, M. pierucciae* and *M. lakamora* become very deepbodied after about one and a half year. They may become nearly as high as long and are very attractive.

Rainbowfishes

Other *Melanotaenia*-groups

Several of the Australian and New Guinean rainbowfish can not be classified into one of the groups outlined above. Species like *Melanotaenia fredericki* or *M. irianjaya* with their different fin shapes and the more slender bodies have to be named here as well as the slender Pima Rainbowfish *M. pimaensis* (which eventually may form a group together with *M. oktediensis)* or *M. parva* which attains a length of only 6 cm. Another exception with no similarity to any other rainbowfish is *M. vanheurni* which attains a length of at least 20 cm in nature. It had been imported but disappeared again.

The genus *Chilatherina*

The genus *Chilatherina,* endemic to New Guinea, is relatively uniform. The fish are rather elongated until an age of about one year with an extraordinary pointed snout, before they start to become more deepbodied. In nearly all species the females show less colour and therefore are not easy to distinghuish from each other. This is the reason why the combination of more than one *Chilatherina* species in an aquarium is not recommended.
There have been a few irritations about the specific identity of *Chilatherina fasciata* and *C. sentaniensis.* Specimens of *C. fasciata* which have been caught in Lake Sentani have been kept for a longer time under the name of *C. sentaniensis* in aquaria. The "real" *C. sentaniensis* or Sentani Rainbowfish originates however from the tributaries to the lake and is noticably more slender than *C. fasciata* (see p. 36; more varieties and species are shown in detail in the AQUALOG-Lexicon). In the natural habitat *C. sentaniensis* lives between rocks in fast flowing water.
However, surely a few specimens will also enter the lake voluntarily or are washed into the lake. Immediately the question arises why there are no crosses of these two closely related species. One possible explanation was given by Gary Lange recently. It seems as if the Lake Sentani Rainbowfishes (although this name should better be given to *C. fasciata)* spawn on leaves or other objects directly under or even below the water surface while *C. fasciata* doesn't use these areas at all.
Another species worth mentioning is *Chilatherina campsi.* It is the only New Guinean rainbowfish species which occurs on both sides of the central mountains (see map p. 13). For the other species this seems to be an invincible barrier to the spread of the species.

The genus *Glossolepis*

In this genus which is also endemic to New Guinea two groups may be distinguished.

Glossolepis incisus-group

This is a group of larger rainbowfishes with a robust body which become very deepbodied when older. They also have large to very large fins *(G. wanamensis,* p. 41, *G.* spec. "Lake Kli", p. 25). Because of their striking colours they are attractive fishes. However, according to the length they can attain in the hobbyist's aquarium – the Salmonred Rainbowfish, *G. incisus,* may grow larger than 20 cm in suitable aquaria – they need very large aquaria.

Glossolepis maculosus-group

The two species in this group, *G. maculosus* and *G. ramuensis,* stay clearly smaller than the other Glossolepis species. They don't attain a length longer than 7 and 9 cm, respectively. However, despite their moderate length and the bright colours they have remained rare in aquarist's tanks.

Further rainbowfishes

Four more genera of rainbowfishes are monotypic, i. e. consist of only a single species. Among these the Threadfin Rainbowfish *Iriatherina werneri,* and the Ornate Rainbowfish *Rhadinocentrus ornatus,* are popular aquarium fishes. There are attempts to place the Threadfin rainbowfish into a subfamily of its own, the Iriatherininae.

Family Pseudomugilidae – Blue-eyes

In the blue-eyes three subfamilies are distinguished which are clearly differentiated from each other. In one of the subfamilies – Pseudomugilinae – further groups may be separated.

Subfamily Kiunginae

According to unconfirmed reports there shall be a second species in addition to the so long only described species – *Kiunga ballochi* – which has been caught and bred by a Hawaiian aquarist. However, nothing more is known and no photos or detailed descriptions seem to exist.

The Fishes
Other Atheriniform Fishes

Subfamily Scaturiginichthyinae

Scaturiginichthys vermeilipinnis is the name of the only species known until today in this subfamily. The name means "redfinned fish from the springs". These blue-eyes originate – in contrast to all other blue-eyes – from pools in the inner part of Australia. The maintenance of captive populations has proven to be very difficult.

Subfamily Pseudomugilinae
– *Pseudomugil furcatus*-group

This group contains only the two species *P. furcatus* and *P. connieae*. When describing the latter species Gerald ALLEN also described a new genus for these two species, *Popondetta*. But as he soon after learned there already was a beetle genus with this name and no name is allowed to be repeated for a genus in the zoological system. Thus he changed the name to *Popondichthys* before the two species were finally placed into the genus *Pseudomugil* because of the larger morphological similarities with the rest of the genus. But as the first introduction of these species into the hobby occurred at the time when the name Popondetta was still valid it persisted in some parts of the literature – incorrectly. The Forktail Blue-eye with a maximum length of 7 cm is arguably the largest representative of the whole genus.

Pseudomugil gertrudae-group

The 2 smaller (up to 3 cm) but very attractive species *P. gertrudae* and *P. paskai* belong to this group.

Pseudomugil signifer-group

The members of this group normally have strikingly attractive coloured dorsal fins. The second dorsal fin is nearly always visible while the first one – also very colourful one – may normally only be seen during mating and displaying.

Pseudomugil tenellus-group

Most blue-eyes belonging to this group show – except when mating – more inconspicuous colours.

Family Telmatherinidae
– Celebes Rainbowfishes

Marosatherina-group

In 1998 AARN, IVANTSOFF and KOTTELAT described the new genus *Marosatherina* for the species which had been introduced to Germany originally in 1935 and which had been described by the Berlin ichthyologist Ernst AHL as *Telmatherina ladigesi*. Although there are a lot of phenotypical similarities with the Australian Threadfin Rainbowfish *Iriatherina werneri*, these two species are not as closely related to each other as the Threadfin Rainbowfish is related to the other rainbowfishes. However, there are more similarities to the only representative of this family found outside Sulawesi, the New Guinean (found on Misool and Batanta Island) *Kalyptatherina helodes*. This is the only known case that a freshwater fish family is found on both sides of the so-called Weber's line, a zoo-geographical separation line between Australia/ New Guinea and the Indonesian islands.

Telmatherina-group

The other species of the genus *Telmatherina* don't have a very detailed aquaristic history.

Family Bedotiidae
– Madagascar Rainbowfishes

The systematic position of this family is not totally clear at present. For some time seen as a family on its own, there is a tendency to recognize these fishes endemic to Madagascar only as members of a subfamily of the Melanotaeniidae. Not only is morphological data used to argue this proposal but it is also possibile to cross the genus *Bedotia* with *Melanotaenia*. However, there is no written report yet as to whether the offspring are fertile or not. There is much evidence that the Bedotiidae and the Melanotaeniidae have a common ancestor. The groups within this family are the two genera *Bedotia* and *Rheocles* (including *Rheocloides*). *Rheocles* species are somewhat more robust while the *Bedotia* species seem to be more slender. The Madagascar Rainbowfish we keep was originally identified under the name *B. geayi*, however, it is possible that the species determination has been wrong and that this fish really belongs to another species. More details on that in the AQUALOG-Lexicon.

Regarding keeping and breeding, the requirements of *Bedotia* species are rather similar to the larger melanotaeniid species. Their breeding is not really difficult. *Rheocles* on the other hand cause us more problems and possibly do not tolerate higher temperatures for the long-term maintenance. To keep them temperatures between 18°C (64°F) and 22°C (72°F) are recommended.

Not yet fully grown male of Chilatherina fasciata from Clearwater Creek. (Photo: N. Armstrong)

Male of the „real" Chilatherina sentaniensis. (Photo: G. W. Lange)

left: Glossolepis ramuensis, semi-adult. (Photo: N. Armstrong)

upper right: Cairnsichthys rhombosomoides.
lower right: Rhadinocentrus ornatus, xanthoristic specimen. (Photos: Hieronimus)

Atherinidae – Atherinid fishes

Until now only a few of the Australian atherinid fishes of the genus *Craterocephalus* have had an aquaristic career in their life history. Many of these prefer harder water. As they often originate from fast flowing and cooler waters they accordingly shouldn't be kept too warm in the aquarium.

One problem with many atherinid fishes is their sensitivity to being caught and exposed to the air. If you catch them in nature with a normal net and put them at once into a bucket or plastic bag in most cases it's already too late and the fishes die. These fishes should be captured with a net and then, while still under water, caught with a suitable container, without touching even the scales or mucosa. Adding a small amount of salt (sodium chloride) to the capture water has been shown to successfully reduce the incidence of death from capture shock. Once transport to the

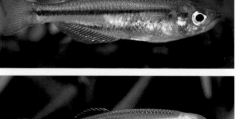

The Fishes
Other Atheriniform Fishes

Wildcaught male of Glossolepis multisquamatus. (Photo: G. R. Allen)

Pseudomugil connieae, Connies Blue-eye. (Photo: G. Schmida)

aquarium has been made successfully their maintenance is a minor problem.

While we know that the *Craterocephalus* species may be bred like the rainbowfishes there are no reports for the other atherinid fishes. As far as we know from the available breeding reports of *Craterocephalus* with the special example of the Blackmast, *C. stramineus* (p. 14), the most attractive representative of the genus, the experiences are contradictory and vary from easy to breed (reports from some Australian breeders) up to very difficult to breed (experiences of many European breeders). *C. stercusmuscarum,* the Fly-specked Hardyhead (see poster), which got its name because of the fine speckles all over the body, and the Strawmast which received its name because of its black first dorsal fin which nearly always is carried erected, are imported from time to time.

upper left: Craterocephalus cf. lacustris. lower left: Telmatherina cf. celebensis.

right: Telmatherina cf. wahjui (Photos: H. Hieronimus)

Local varieties

As already mentioned before the rainbowfishes are a relatively young family according to our present knowledge – speaking in evolutionary terms. But not only are there species and subspecies but also there are many local varieties which – according to the place where they were found – show differences in colour and patterning and sometimes also morphology, which seem to be too small to place them even into suspecific rank. In the AQUALOG-Lexicon "all atherinids" nearly all of the varieties we currently know are depicted, therefore the problem is only mentioned here.

Because of the differences between the local varieties it is necessary to keep them in your aquarium not only with their genus and specific name (and maybe additionally the common name) but also under the locality name. That's most important if you distribute your offspring. Accordingly *Melanotaenia trifasciata* "Goyder River" is kept and bred under exactly this name by many breeders. Only with the locality name added the purchaser is enabled to get a true understanding of what he's going to buy, as many rainbowfishes are sold as semi-adult fishes and don't show their mature colours. As you will see in the AQUALOG-Lexicon and from what is only briefly outlined in this book several varieties with very different colours could be confused if you only use the specific name.

By the way, the colour varieties are distinguished from crosses by the fact that the offsping are absolutely identical to their parents. Even after several generations they still show their typical colours.

Melanotaeniidae – Rainbowfishes

Some rainbowfishes especially show a larger number of local varieties. This may be caused by their large distribution area as well as the occurrence of some species in Australia as well as in New Guinea. For some species you can literally speak of a local variety for every river, and in larger rivers local varieties have been distinguished from the major tributaries as well as parts of the same river e. g. upper and lower sections.

In *Melanotaenia splendida* this has already lead to the erection of four subspecies in Australia. Factually we also find transition areas between the subspecies, and also within the area of each subspecies we can distinguish between several local varieties. In the distribution area of *M. splendida* there are many remote areas which haven't yet been collected intensively.

At present about 40 more or less different varieties of *M. trifasciata* are not only documentated but also kept in aquaria. More local varieties are not known from any other species or perhaps the differences between the local varieties are not as marked. Maybe all the different populations of *M. trifasciata* had contact until the last ice-age when the sea level was significantly lower and most of the rivers flowed into the Arafura Sea. The isolation of these populations after the flooding of the Arafura Sea and the Gulf of Carpentaria by rising sea levels possibly initiated the species evolution which still is in progress. However, according to what we know today there are not just rivers which have their own variety but there may be also differences between populations which occur in different parts of larger rivers or in their tributaries. So the Goyder River drainage is at least inhabited by two different colour varieties (see p. 40).

Melanotaenia maccullochi and *Iriatherina werneri* are two species which occur in Australia as well as in New Guinea. However, the Dwarf Rainbowfish shows several local varieties (p. 40), mostly originating from Australia, which are shown in the AQUALOG-Lexicon in detail.

Most of the rainbowfishes found in New Guinea have a rather small spread. Maybe these populations were already isolated for a longer time. As far as we know today only *Chilatherina fasciata* and *Melanotaenia affinis* show several local varieties – one is depictured on p. 33 –, surely more exist. There may also be a variety of *Glossolepis multisquamatus* as the fish known from Lake Kli, which is fed by the Mamberamo River, belongs to this species (p. 25).

Pseudomugilidae –Blue-eyes

There are also several varieties known from the blue-eyes, which apply to their colouration as well as to the fin shape. Often – but not always – it seems the blue-eyes which occur in waters with noticable salt content show the elongated dorsal fins in males. It is difficult to obtain these fins in the offspring, possibly a salt addition may be necessary.

The Fishes
Breeding Forms and Threatened Species

Telmatherinidae – Celebes Rainbowfishes

Most of the *Telmatherina* species (except *T. bonti*) are rather similar to each other and sometimes co-occur in the same lake, But if they are just varieties of one or a few very variable species (or relatively young species) must be ascertained in further examinations. In this situation perhaps aquarists can help to solve this question by breeding the species.

Bedotiidae – Madagascar Rainbowfishes

Until recently there seemed to be no uncertainty about these fishes. But imports from various habitats in the last few years with slight but visible differences between the fishes lead to the conclusion that there may be also local varieties in the *Bedotia* species. For more details see the AQUALOG-Lexicon.

Breeding forms

Although the aquaristic history of the rainbowfishes is still relatively short there already exist a few breeding forms. From *Iriatherina werneri* (see poster) as well as from *Rhadinocentrus ornatus* (p. 36) we know xanthoristic specimens which totally lack the black colours and whose bodies have a fleshy colour. In *Glossolepis incisus* there are partially xanthoristic specimens which are called "marbled" (see poster). All these breeding forms resulted from gene mutations, i. e. sudden gene changes.

By selection some breeding forms of *Melanotaenia boesemani* have been developed (p. 40). To do that breeders have used the natural variability of the red colouration of the posterior part of the male bodies and thus selected for red and yellow strains.

Breeding forms do have their justification. But it is important that you don't pass them on to other aquarists or to the trade with a locality or species name but – correctly – as breeding forms.

ENDANGERED SPECIES

Although parts of Australia as well as New Guinea belong to the most remote and unapproachable parts of the world even there species have become extinct or are becoming threatened and endangered.

Melanotaenia eachamensis

In the early 80s there were only 23 specimens left in the hands of private aquarists of this fish which formerly had occured in Lake Eacham in Queensland. In the natural habitat they became extinct as the result of the release of a predatory fish. With some of these fishes left today's numerous stocks in public and private aquaria have been built.

Recent genetic examinations have demonstrated that several varieties from biotopes close to Lake Eacham belong to *M. eachamensis*. However, as they clearly show external differences the results are doubtful – in my personal opinion. At least the population originating directly from Lake Eacham has to be conserved in any case and these others considered as local varieties.

Glossolepis wanamensis

When Heiko BLEHER in 1995 again visited Lake Wanam, he was confronted with the fact that there were only a few adult specimens left from the former millions of rainbowfish. In total he caught seven adults, no fry or semi-adults. On the other hand he saw millions of Tilapia cichlids which had been released there. That's the reason why one of the most beautiful rainbowfishes will become extinct in its natural habitat. That makes it even more important to conserve this species in aquaria.

Melanotaenia ajamaruensis

Since its first description this fish, originating from the Lakes Ajamaru where it co-occurred with *M. boesemani,* hasn't been found again. Thus it is registered as missing.

Melanotaenia oktediensis

Parts of the Oktedi River are heavily polluted by mine wastes and although the distribution area of this species is not affected yet this species is at least potentially threatened.

Bedotiidae

All *Bedotia* and especially *Rheocles* species have to be considered as potentially threatened by severe nature devastation and competition from introduced feral species on Madagascar.

The Fishes
Local Varietis and Breeding Forms

Melanotaenia maccullochi
left: Skull Creek, Cape York.
right: Southeast part of Cape York, both in Australia.
(Photos: N. Armstrong)

Melanotaenia trifasciata
left: Pappin Creek (don't confuse it with M. herbertaxelrodi!).
(Photo: N. Armstrong)
right: from Goyder River tributary.
(Photo: G. Maebe)
Goyder River s. pp. 2/3

Melanotaenia trifasciata
left: Upper Coen River, pair, male on top.
(Photo: G. W. Lange)
right: Coen River, male.
(Photo: G. Maebe)

Melanotaenia splendida australis
left: Drysdale River, Kimberley, Western Australia.
right: Blackmore River, Northern Territory.
(Photos: G. Schmida)

Melanotaenia boesemani
left: breeding variety yellow.
(Photo: E. Schraml)
right: breeding variety red.
(Photo: R. Kuiter)

The Fishes
Threatened Species

above: Male Glossolepis wanamensis, 140 mm long. Bred specimens must not have red fins (crosses)! (Photo: N. Armstrong)

left: Pair of Melanotaenia eachamensis in normal colouration, male on the left. (Photo: H. Hieronimus)

left: Male Melanotaenia eachamensis in mating colours. (Photo: N. Armstrong)

right: Male Melanotaenia oktediensis. (Photo: G. Maebe)

AQUALOG Lexicon

The **AQUALOG** team has set itself the goal to catalogue all known ornamental fishes of the world – and this task will, of course, take several years, as there are over 40,000 fish species.

Compiling an **AQUALOG**lexicon, we take a certain group of fishes, label all known species with code-numbers, look for the newest results of fish research about natural distribution, features and maintenance of the fishes and try to get the best photographs, often from the most remote parts of the world.

Our ingenious code-number-system labels every species with its own individual code-number which the fish keeps even if a scientific re-naming occurs.

And not only the species gets a number, also each variety, distinguishing locality, colour, and breeding form.

This system makes every fish absolutely distinct for everybody. With it, international communication is very easy, because a simple number crosses almost all language barriers.

This is an advantage not only for dealers, but for hobbyists, too, and thus for all people involved in the aquarium hobby.

Again and again, new fish species are discovered or new varieties bred. Consequently, the number of fishes assigned to a certain group changes constantly and information from available specialist literature is only reliable within certain time limits. Thus, an identification lexicon that is up-to-date today is outdated after as little as one year.

To give aquarists an identification 'tool' that stays up-to-date for many years, we developed our ingenious patented code-number system.

When going to press, our books contain all fishes that are known to that date. All newly discovered or bred species are regularly published as either supplements or as so-called "stickups" in **AQUALOG**news.

These supplementary peel-back stickers can be attached to the empty pages in the back of the books.

As you can see, we provide the latest information from specialists for hobbyists. Over the years, your **AQUALOG** books will 'grow' to a complete encyclopaedia on ornamental fishes, a beautiful lexicon that is never outdated and easy to use.

AQUALOGnews

AQUALOGnews is the first international newspaper for aquarists, published in four-colour print, available in either German or English language and full of the latest news from the aquatic world.

The following rubrics are included:Top Ten, Brand New, Evergreens, Technics, Terraristics, Fish Doctor and Flora. Further, there are travel accounts, breeding reports, stories about new and well-known fish etc.

The news gives us the opportunity to be up-to-date, because up to one week before going to press, we can include reports and the 'hottest' available information.

This way, every six weeks a newspaper for friends of the aquarium hobby is published that makes sure to inform you about the latest 'arrivals' waiting for you at your local pet shop.

AQUALOGnews can be subscribed to and contains 40 supplementary stickers for your AQUALOG books in 12 issues. You can subscribe to the news either via your local pet shop or directly at the publishers.

Issues without stickups (print run: 80,000) are available at well-sorted pet shops. The newspaper also informs you about newly published supplements.

AQUALOG *Special*

The *Specials* series is not intended to repeat all the things that were already known twenty years ago, like 'how to build your own aquarium' – something, probably nobody practises anymore, because there is no need to do so.

We provide the latest and most important information on fish keeping and tending: precisely and easily understandable.

We want to offer advice that helps you to avoid mistakes – and help your fishes to live a healthy life.

We intend to win more and more friends for our beautiful and healthy (because stress-reducing!) hobby.

Order our new free catalogue, where all our previous books and the ones in preparation are shown and described.

Did this book make you curious? You want to learn all about the different forms and varieties of the wonderful and exciting Rainbowfishes?

You'll find them **all** in the Aqualog-Lexicon „All Rainbowfishes " including breeding varieties, colour- and local varieties! Always with colour photograph, international symbols and the Aqualog - Codenumber.

With the supplements that are released regularly, your Aqualog - Lexicon will stay up-to-date for years! (ISBN: 3-931702-80-4)

MORE INTERESTING *SPECIALS* :

ISBN: 3-931702-69-3

ISBN: 3-931702-41-3

ISBN: 3-931702-39-1

ISBN: 3-931702-34-0

ISBN: 3-931702-49-9

ISBN: 3-931702-53-7

ISBN: 3-931702-43-X

ISBN: 3-931702-45-6

UPCOMING *SPECIALS:*

Southamerican Freshwater Stingrays
Decorative Aquaria: A Marine Tank for Beginners
Precious Little Jewels – Goodeids
Decorative Aquaria: The Dutch Waterplant Tank
Freshwater Coral Fish – Tanganjika
The Colourful World of Livebearers

Order your free specimen copy of **AQUALOG***news* and the new **AQUALOG** programme!

For latest informations and new released books see internet:

http://www.aqualog.de or contact the publisher directly:

AQUALOG Verlag, Liebigstr. 1, D-63110 Rodgau
Tel.: +49 (0) 06106 - 69 01 40
Fax: +49 (0) 06106 - 64 46 92
E-Mail: acs@aqualog.de

above: Melanotaenia rubripinnis

lower left: Habitat of M. rubripinnis, G. leggetti and C. alleni near Siewa, IJ.

On the right: above: Chilatherina alleni. below: Glossolepis leggetti. (Photos: G. R. Allen)

New species and outlook

During recent times nearly every year new species of rainbowfishes have been discovered. There are still several parts of New Guinea which haven't yet been examined. According to current trends there are still more species to be detected. That doesn't just affect the rainbowfishes but also the blue-eyes.

Even in Australia discoveries are still possible. Some areas are so remote that they may only be reached with great difficulty. The mouth of the Prince Regent River, home of *M. pygmaea*, is not just inhabited by sharks but also by far more dangerous saltwater crocodiles which may reach a length of more than 7 m. Whoever wants to catch his own fish has to be very careful in some areas.

The Fishes
New Species

Melanotaenia caerulea.

A new variety of
Melanotaenia praecox,
discovered in 1997 in
the vicinity of Siewa,
Irian Jaya.
(Photos: G. R. Allen)

But even from the more accessible parts of Australia we know of several *Melanotaenia* varieties which may not be with certainty identified as a known species. Much work is still left for the ichthyologists.

Unfortunately none of the species shown on these two pages have made their way yet to Australia, the USA or into Europe. But some of them are already in a New Guinean aquarium just waiting to be picked up by somebody coming along.

*Pseudomugil pellucidus,
a blue-eye described in
1997.*

LITERATURE:

ALLEN, G.R. (1989):
Freshwater Fishes of Australia.
T.F.H. Publications, Neptune City

ALLEN, G.R. (1991):
Field Guide to the Freshwater Fishes
of New Guinea.
Christensen Research Institute Publications No. 9,
Madang, Papua-Neuguinea

ALLEN, G. R. (1995):
Rainbowfishes in nature and home.
Tetra Press, Melle

ALLEN, G.R. & N. J. Cross (1982):
Rainbowfishes of Australia and
Papua New Guinea.
T.F.H. Publications, Neptune City

BASSLEER, G. (1996):
Bildatlas der Fischkrankheiten
im Süßwasseraquarium.
distributed by:
Verlag A.C.S., Liebigstr. 1, D-63110 Rodgau

HIERONIMUS, H. (1997):
Ihr Hobby: Regenbogenfische.
bede-Verlag, Ruhmannsfelden

LARSON, H.K. & K.C. MARTIN (1990):
Freshwater Fishes
of the Northern Territory.
Northern Territory Museum Handbook
Series No. 1, Darwin

LEGGETT, R., & J.R. MERRICK (1987):
Australian Native Fishes for Aquaria.
J. R. Merrick Publications, Sydney

NOGA, E.J. (1995):
Fish Disease: Diagnosis and Treatment.
Mosby Year-Book, Inc., St. Louis

SCHMIDA, G. (1998): Regenbogenfische.
Gräfe & Unzer Verlag, München

SCHUBERT, P. (1991):
Urania Ratgeber Aquarium: Regenbogenfische.
Urania-Verlag, Leipzig

UNTERGASSER, D. (1989):
Krankheiten der Aquarienfische:
Diagnose und Behandlung.
Kosmos-Verlag, Stuttgart

MAGAZINES:

"Rainbowfish"
quarterly journal of the International Rainbowfish
Association. Since 1986.
Issued in German, English and Dutch.
Contact address: H. Hieronimus,
P.O.Box 170209, D-42624 Solingen

„Fishes of Sahul"
Quarterly magazine of the Australia
New Guinea Fishes Association
Contact address:
ANGFA,
P.O. Box 240, Strathpine 4500, Australia

„Rainbow Times"
bimonthly journal of the
Rainbowfish Study Group (USA)
Contact address:
Sherry Taylor,
171 Campbell Lane, Cookville, TN 38501, U.S.A.

aqua
Journal of Ichthyology and Aquatic Biology
supplement to aqua-geographia
Aquapress, Graffignana (Lody), Italien

Ichthyological Exploration of Freshwaters
quarterly, Verlag Dr. Friedrich Pfeil, Munich

Revue francaise d'aquariologie
herpetologiequarterly, Nancy, France

GLOSSARY:

Endemic: Occuring solely in a certain, restricted area.

Genetic plasticity: A high rate of mutations in the gene pool which may cause the fast development of species or varieties.

Group: Similar species with close genetic relationship.

Ichthyology: Science of fishes

Local variety: Different coloured only locally found variety of a more widespread species. If a variety is considered as just a variety or given subspecies or species rank is up to the researcher and not obligatory.

Morphology: Description of the outer features (fin rays, scales, vertebrae, bodyshape, etc.)

Mutations: Spontaneous changes of genes.

Species: Defined as representative of a geographically isolated, self reproducing fish community. The definition is not very strict and there may be differences about a species rank among different researchers. This is the explanation for descrepancies in the nomination of species.

Systematics: Description of the relations of the fish among each other (and arrangement in species, genera, families, etc.).

Index

name	poster, page
aeromonas	29
allergy	18
antibiotics	29, 30
ants	18
Aponogeton madagascariensis	16
Arafura sea	12, 38
Atherinidae	9, 12, 14, 35
Atheriniformes	8, 9, 31
Atherinoidea	9
Atherinomorpha	9
Bedotia	14, 17, 35, 39
Bedotia cf. geayi	8, 21, 35
Bedotia cf. madagascariensis	H-8, 21
Bedotiidae	8, 9, 12, 14, 35, 39
blue-eye, forktail	G-7, 24, 35
blue-eye, pacific	B-8, 8, 10, 11, 26, 35
brine shrimp naupliae	18, 19, 23, 26
Cairnsichthys	9
Cairnsichthys rhombosomoides	36
Camallanus cotti	30
Chilatherina	9, 20, 27, 34
Chilatherina alleni	44
Chilatherina axelrodi	A-1
Chilatherina bleheri	B-1, 33
Chilatherina campsi	34
Chilatherina fasciata	C-1, 34, 36, 38
Chilatherina sentaniensis	D-1, 34, 36
Columnaris	29
Craterocephalus	8, 12, 14, 20, 36
Craterocephalus cf. lacustris	37
Craterocephalus stercusmuscarum	G-8, 37
Craterocephalus stramineus	14, 37
crosses	21, 23, 41
Dentatherinidae	12
desinfection	27
disease, velvet	28, 30
diseases, acid and alkali	30
drosophila	18
fish tuberculosis	29
Glossolepis	9, 34
Glossolepis cf. multisquamatus	A-2
Glossolepis incisus	E-1, F-1, 10, 14, 21, 34, 39
Glossolepis leggetti	44
Glossolepis maculosus	G-1, 34
Glossolepis multisquamatus	H-1, 14, 37, 38
Glossolepis ramuensis	34, 36
Glossolepis sp. "Lake Kli"	25, 34
Glossolepis wanamensis	B-2, 34, 39, 41
hardyhead, fly-specked	G-8, 37
hardyheads	8, 12, 14, 20, 36
Harvey Creek	11, 26
Heteranthera zosterifolia	16
Howard Swamps	17
hybrids	21, 23, 41
Ich	27, 28
Ichthyophthiriasis	27, 28
Ichthyophthirius multifiliis	27, 28
infections, bacterial	29
IRG	6, 11
Iriatherina	9
Iriatherina werneri	C-2, D-2, 6, 10, 18, 19, 20, 34, 35, 38, 39
Iriatherininae	34
Kalyptatherina helodes	35
Kiunga	9
Kiunga ballochi	34
Kiunginae	9, 34
lemna	18
malachit green oxalate	28
Marosatherina	17, 35
Marosatherina ladigesi	F-8, 8, 14, 35
Melanotaenia	9, 34, 35
Melanotaenia affinis	E-2, F-2, G-2, 31, 38
Melanotaenia affinis "Pagwi"	33
Melanotaenia ajamaruensis	39
Melanotaenia arfakensis	A-3, H-2
Melanotaenia boesemani	B-3, C-3, 6, 9, 11, 15, 20, 26, 31, 39, 40
Melanotaenia caerulea	31, 45
Melanotaenia cf. exquisita	32
Melanotaenia duboulayi	D-3, 10, 31
Melanotaenia eachamensis	E-3, 31, 39, 41
Melanotaenia exquisita	F-3, 31
Melanotaenia fluviatilis	G-3, 31
Melanotaenia fredericki	H-3, 34
Melanotaenia goldiei	A-4, 31, 32
Melanotaenia gracilis	B-4, 31
Melanotaenia "greeti"	21
Melanotaenia "hammeri"	21
Melanotaenia herbertaxelrodi	C-4, 6, 24, 31, 40
Melanotaenia irianjaya	D-4, 34
Melanotaenia kamaka	E-4, 32, 33
Melanotaenia lacustris	F-4, 8, 11, 15, 26, 28, 31
Melanotaenia lakamora	G-4, 33
Melanotaenia maccullochi	H-4, 10, 31, 38, 40
Melanotaenia "marci"	21
Melanotaenia misoolensis	33
Melanotaenia monticola	A-5, 31
Melanotaenia nigrans	B-5, 8, 9, 10, 14, 17, 31
Melanotaenia oktediensis	C-5, 34, 39, 41
Melanotaenia papuae	D-5, 31
Melanotaenia parkinsoni	E-5, F-5, 31
Melanotaenia parva	34
Melanotaenia pierucciae	G-5, 33
Melanotaenia pimaensis	34
Melanotaenia praecox	H-5, 11, 17, 20, 21, 33, 45
Melanotaenia pygmaea	A-6, 44
Melanotaenia rubripinnis	44
Melanotaenia sexlineata	B-6, 31
Melanotaenia sp. „Batanta"	33
Melanotaenia splendida	12, 31, 38
Melanotaenia splendida australis	C-6, 13, 17, 31
Melanotaenia splendida australis Blackmore River	40
Melanotaenia splendida australis Drysdale River	40
Melanotaenia splendida inornata	D-6, 15
Melanotaenia splendida rubrostriata	G-6, 31
Melanotaenia splendida splendida	E-6, F-6
Melanotaenia trifasciata	12, 22, 29, 31, 38
Melanotaenia trifasciata, Burster Creek	25
Melanotaenia trifasciata, Coen River	H-6, 40
Melanotaenia trifasciata, Giddy River	A-7
Melanotaenia trifasciata, Goyder River	B-7, 2/3, 13, 17, 38
Melanotaenia trifasciata, Goyder River-tributary	40
Melanotaenia trifasciata, Pappin Creek	40
Melanotaenia trifasciata, Wonga Creek	32
Melanotaenia trifasciata, Yirrkala	29
Melanotaenia vanheurni	34
Melanotaeniidae	8, 9, 12, 31, 35, 38
methylene blue	23, 28
mosquito larvae, red	18
mycobacterium	29
Oodinium pillularis	28
parasites, intestinal	30
Pelangia	9
Phallostethidae	12
poisoning	30
poisoning, nitrite	28, 30
Popondetta	28, 35
Popondichthys	35
Pseudomugil	9, 26
Pseudomugil connieae	E-7, 28, 35, 37
Pseudomugil cyanodorsalis	F-7, 26
Pseudomugil furcatus	G-7, 24, 35
Pseudomugil gertrudae	H-7, 35
Pseudomugil mellis	A-8
Pseudomugil paskai	35
Pseudomugil pellucidus	45
Pseudomugil signifer	B-8, 8, 10, 11, 26, 35
Pseudomugil tenellus	C-8, 17, 35
Pseudomugilidae	8, 9, 12, 34, 38
quarantine-aquarium	27
Rainbowfish, Black-banded	B-5, 8, 9, 10, 14, 17, 31
Rainbowfish, Bleher's	B-1, 33
Rainbowfish, Boeseman's	B-3, C-3, 6, 9, 11, 15, 20, 26, 31, 39, 40
Rainbowfish, Burster Creek	25
Rainbowfish, Celebes	F-8, 8, 14, 35
Rainbowfish, Dwarf	H-4, 10, 31, 38, 40
Rainbowfish, Fly river	B-6, 31
Rainbowfish, Goyder River	B-7, 2/3, 13, 17, 19, 38
Rainbowfish, Lake Eacham	E-3, 31, 39, 41
Rainbowfish, Mountain	A-5, 31
Rainbowfish, Neon	H-5, 11, 17, 20, 21, 33, 45
Rainbowfish, Papua	D-5, 31
Rainbowfish, Parkinsons	E-5, F-5, 31
Rainbowfish, Red-striped	G-6, 31
Rainbowfish, Salmonred	E-1, F-1, 10, 14, 21, 34, 39
Rainbowfish, Sentani	D-1, 34, 36
Rainbowfish, Threadfin	C-2, D-2, 6, 10, 18, 19, 20, 34, 35, 38, 39
Rainbowfish, Wonga Creek	32
Rainbowfish, Yirrkala	29
Rhadinocentrus ornatus	C-7, D-7, 34, 36, 39
Rheocles	14, 35, 39
Roper River	17
Scaturiginichthyinae	9, 35
Scaturiginichthys	9
Scaturiginichthys vermeilipinnis	14, 35
Siewa	44, 45
spawning mop	22
spawning substrate	16, 22, 23
strawmast	14, 37
Telmatherina	15, 20, 35, 39
Telmatherina antoniae	D-8
Telmatherina bonti	39
Telmatherina cf. celebensis	37
Telmatherina cf. sarasinorum	E-8
Telmatherina cf. wahjui	37
Telmatherina ladigesi	35
Telmatherinidae	9, 12, 15, 35, 39
ulcers	28
Vesicularia dubyana	16
Vibrio	29
Vibriosis	29
vinegar eels	19
water lenses	18
Whitespot disease	27, 28
worm, grindal	18
worm, micro	19
worm, tillerhead	30
worm, white	18

> **Bold printed characters/numbers show the place on the attached poster!**

Symbols

Continent of origin:

Simply check the letter in front of the code-number

A = Africa   **E** = Europe   **N** = North America

S = South + Central America   **X** = Asia + Australia

Age:

the last number of the code always stands
for the age of the fish in the photo:

1 = small   (baby, juvenile colouration)
2 = medium   (young fish / saleable size)
3 = large   (half-grown / good saleable size)
4 = XL   (fully grown / adult)
5 = XXL   (brooder)
6 = show   (show-fish)

Immediate origin:

W = wild
B = bred
Z = breeding-form
X = crossbreed

Size:

..cm = approximate size these fish can reach as
adults

Sex:

♂ male   ♀ female   ♂♀ pair

Temperature:

◁ 18-22°C (64 - 72°F) (room temperature)
▷ 22-25°C (72 -77°F) (tropical fish)
△ 24-29°C (75 - 85°F) (Discus etc.)
▽ 10-22°C (50 - 72°F) cold

pH-Value:

P pH 6,5 - 7,2 no special requirements (neutral)
↓P pH 5,8 - 6,5 prefers soft, slightly acidic water
↑P pH 7,5 - 8,5 prefers hard, alkaline water

Lighting:

○ bright, plenty of light / sun
◑ not too bright
● almost dark

Food:

☺ omnivorous / dry food, no special requirements
😐 food specialist, live food / frozen food
☹ predator, feed with live fish
◉ plant-eater, supplement with plant food

Swimming:

⊞ no special characteristics
⬆ in upper area / surface fish
⬇ in lower area / floor fish

Aquarium- set up:

▭ only floor and stones etc.
▨ stones / roots / crevices
▩ plant aquarium + stones / roots

Behaviour / reproduction:

♥ keep a pair or a trio
🐟 school fish, do not keep less than 10
🐟 egg-layer
🐟 livebearer / viviparous
🐟 mouthbrooder
🐟 cavebrooder
🐟 bubblenest-builder
◆ algae-eater, glass-cleaner (roots + spinach)
◈ non aggressive fish, easy to keep (mixed aquarium)
▲ difficult to keep, read specialist literature beforehand
🛑 warning, extremely difficult, for experienced specialists only
❶ the eggs need special care
§ protected species (WA), special license required ("CITES")

Minimum tank: capacity:

⟦ss⟧	super small	20 - 40 cm	5 - 20 l
⟦s⟧	small	40 - 80 cm	40 - 80 l
⟦m⟧	medium	60 - 100 cm	80 - 200 l
⟦l⟧	large	100 - 200 cm	200 - 400 l
⟦xl⟧	XL	200 - 400 cm	400 - 3000 l
⟦xxl⟧	XXL	over 400 cm	over 3000 l
			(show aquarium)

Inches

Centimeter

Key to the abbreviations of the scientific names

Example: ***Belontia signata jonklaasi*** BENL & TEROFAL, 1975
      Genus   Species   Subspecies   Describer , Year of the publication

sp.:   **a species name is not yet available**

sp. aff.:   **similar species**
The species is not yet determined but it is very similar to the
one named in the following

cf.:   **in all probability this species**
The specimen shown or the respective population differs in
some minor details from the typical form, but these differences don't justify to place it into a species of its own.

Hybrid :   **Crossbreed**

ssp.:   **Subspecies**
Explanation: Some species inhabit an area of very wide range;
within this area, there are populations that differ significantly
from other populations in appearance, but seen genetically,
they belong nevertheless to the same species. Those populations get a third scientific name as geographical subspecies.
If a subspecies name has not yet been formally given, the
abbreviation spp. is added.

var. :   **Variation**
Explanation: Individual differences in colour combination,
which are not fixed in geographical areas, are so-called varia-
tions. They do not get a special scientific name.

Intergrade: **Mixed population of two subspecies**